Jewish
REGIONAL COOKING

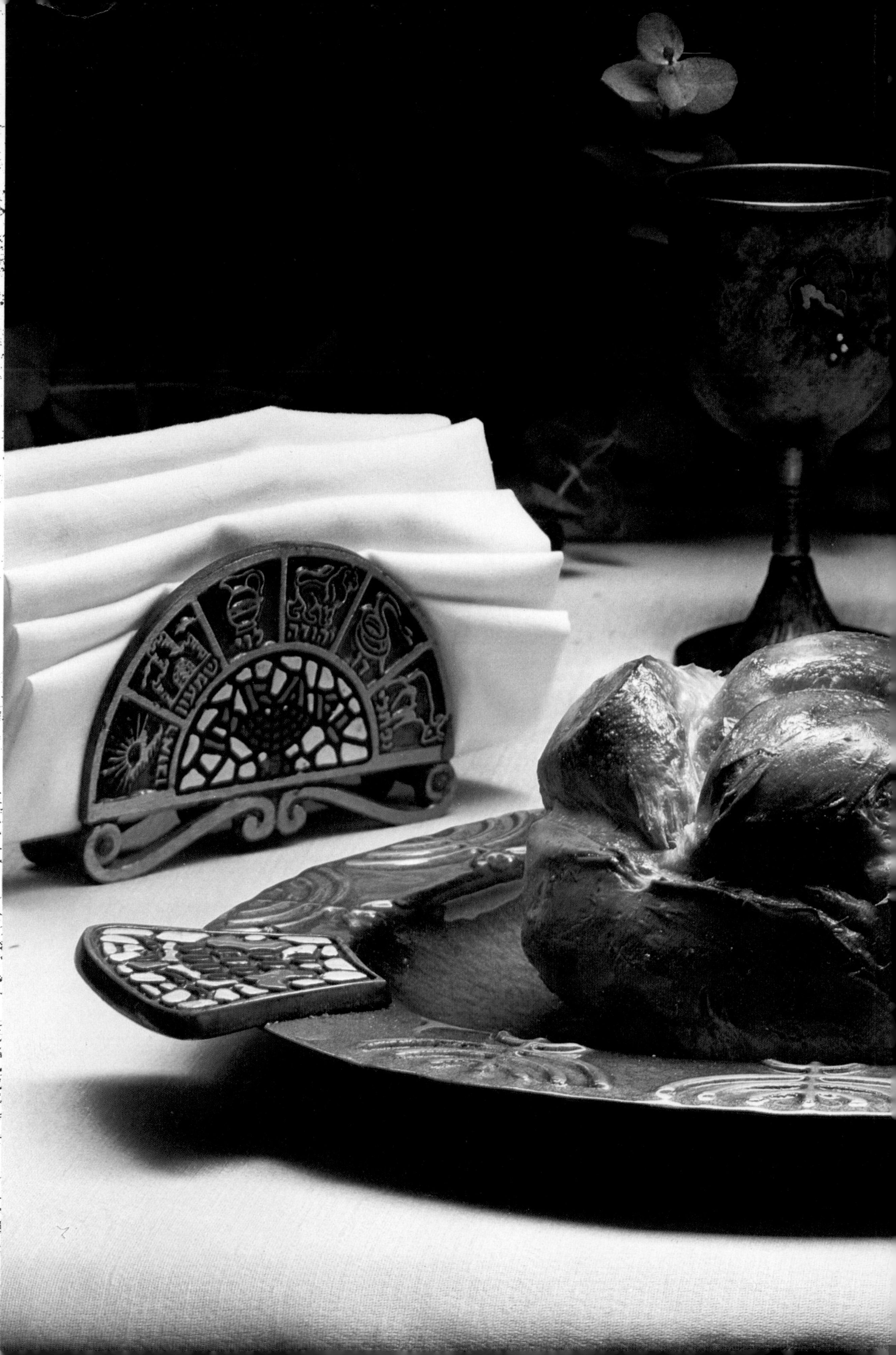

RICHARD HAASE

Jewish
REGIONAL COOKING

Macdonald

A Macdonald Book

Copyright © 1985 Quarto Publishing Ltd

First published in Great Britain in 1985
Published by Macdonald & Co (Publishers) Ltd
London & Sydney
A Member of BPCC plc

British Library Cataloguing in Publication Data
Haase, Richard
  Jewish regional cooking
  1. Cooking, Jewish
  I. Title
  641.5'676   TX274

ISBN 0-356-10780-9

This book was designed and produced by
Quarto Publishing Ltd
The Old Brewery, 6 Blundell Street, London N7 9BH

Senior Editor Jane Rollason
Designer Peter Bridgewater
Illustrator Lorraine Harrison
Food Photography Edward Hing, Janine Norton
Art Editor Moira Clinch

Art Director Alastair Campbell
Editorial Director Jim Miles

Typeset by QV Typesetting Ltd, London
Colour origination by Rainbow Graphic Arts Co Ltd, Hong Kong
Printed by LeeFung-Asco Printers Ltd, Hong Kong

Macdonald & Co (Publishers) Ltd
Maxwell House, 74 Worship Street, London EC2A 2EN

Contents

The diaspora of Jewish culture

The word diaspora comes from the Greek word meaning scattering. It generally refers to the scattering of the Jewish people outside of Israel, a process with ancient origins.

Forty years after their flight from Egypt under the leadership of Moses, the Jews arrived at the promised land of Canaan. Under the leadership of Joshua, they conquered Canaan and established themselves there. By the time of Solomon, about 970 BCE, the Jews had become a cohesive society centred in Israel. Even then, however, Jews lived outside the homeland, in Egypt and elsewhere.

After the Assyrian conquests of Israel in 722 BCE many Jews were dispersed to the east into Persia and the area near the Caspian Sea. The first catastrophic exile of the Jews occurred when Judea fell to the Babylonians and the Temple in Jerusalem was destroyed in 586 BCE. The Jews were exiled from their homeland, with many carried off into captivity in Babylonia. In Babylon they enjoyed a surprising level of prosperity and religious freedom, but still yearned for Israel. The desire to return was fulfilled in 539 BCE, when Babylonia was in turn conquered by Cyrus the Great, King of the Persians. Cyrus, the founder of the Persian Empire, issued a proclamation allowing the Jews to return to their homeland and permitting them to rebuild the Temple. (The new Temple was dedicated in 516 BCE.) Many Jews returned, although many others stayed on in Babylonia and made it an important centre of Jewish culture. By this time there were also significant Jewish communities in Syria, Egypt and Persia.

The Persian Empire lasted until the advent of Alexander the Great. By the time of Alexander's death in 323 BCE, much that had been Persian was now part of his enormous empire.

The Hellenization of the Middle East, which began with Alexander and continued for seven centuries, had enormous significance for the Jews. Greek language, art, philosophy, religion and culture were important influences, particularly for those Jews living outside the Holy Land. The city of Alexandria, founded by Alexander in 332 BCE, was a major centre of Jewish culture for centuries. The Jews there held important positions in the Greek and later in the Roman world. Their synagogue was famed for its beauty.

Foreign rule and foreign religions were less congenial to the Jews still living in Palestine. In the middle of the second century BCE the Jews, under the leadership of Judas Maccabeus, revolted against the despotic rule of Antiochus and established an independent Jewish state in 165 BCE. The victory and the miraculous rededication of the Temple that followed are commemorated on the holiday of Chanuka.

The Hasmonean dynasty founded by Judas was conquered by the Romans in 63 BCE. This brought further dispersal of the Jews from their homeland, but now the

dispersal was not so much eastwards towards Persia (although Jews reached Bombay by 175 BCE) but westwards into Roman Europe, particularly to Rome and Italy. From there, Jews settled in Spain and France, and then in England and Germany. Persecution in Germany forced them into Poland and Russia.

By 750 CE, the Islamic conquest of the Mediterranean was well underway. The Muslims were far more tolerant of the Jews than the Christians were, and Jewish communities flourished in Spain, North Africa and the Middle East. Nevertheless, the Jews still faced discrimination and persecution, conditions that persist into this century in Muslim countries.

The expulsion of the Jews from Spain and Portugal in the fifteenth century scattered them further. Some settled in North Africa, while others went to Amsterdam, Turkey and the New World.

The scattering of the Jews continued over the centuries. It was accelerated once again starting in the 1880s by persecution and political instability in Russia and Eastern Europe. Many Jews emigrated to Western Europe and America at this time.

World War I led to massive dislocations of the Jews and large-scale emigration to America and elsewhere. The Holocaust of World War II virtually destroyed the Jewish communities of Europe. Many of the Jews who survived ̶ ̶zi rule were dispersed to America and to the new state ̶ ̶ael.

ISRAEL & THE ISLAMIC WORLD	FRANCE & ITALY
RUSSIA & EASTERN EUROPE	SPAIN, PORTUGAL & THE NEW WORLD
GERMANY & AUSTRIA	ENGLISH-SPEAKING WORLD

Because of the diaspora of Jewish culture, there is no one style of Jewish cooking. The Jews, wherever they were, adapted the local cuisine to their dietary laws. The diversity of Jewish culture is reflected in the many Jewish cooking styles from different lands.

The modern Jewish kitchen

Jewish cooking is based on the observance of the dietary laws set forth in the Bible and rabbinical ordinanaces. These laws, which are not any longer strictly obeyed in many Jewish households, divide food into permitted and forbidden categories. The permitted foods are popularly called 'kosher', from the Hebrew *kasher*, and the forbidden foods are called 'trayf', from the Hebrew *terefah*.

For meats to be kosher, they must come from an animal that has a cloven hoof, that chews the cud and that has been ritually slaughtered. This means that beef, lamb, veal and even goat are kosher, but that rabbit, for example, is not. Pork is strictly forbidden. Among birds, ritually slaughtered barnyard poultry are generally kosher, but birds of prey and scavengers are not. Seafood must have fins and scales. Eels, shellfish and crustaceans are not kosher.

The blood of animals must not be eaten, and all meat must be well drained and salted before using, which is why liver and all meat is always cooked very thoroughly in Jewish cooking. Animals are slaughtered by a *shochet*, who must be a pious man learned in the law. It is his obligation to kill the animal humanely and to inspect it for disease.

An important part of the dietary laws is the prohibition against mixing milk ('milchig') foods and meat ('fleischig') foods. This dates back to the Biblical injunction against cooking a kid in its mother's milk. Jewish cooking is filled with ingenious ways of complying with this prohibition. In modern times, the development of non-dairy cream substitute, soybean-based ice-cream and milk, pure vegetable margarines and even artificial bacon bits, has been a boon to kosher cooks. Some of the recipes in this book can be prepared using non-kosher methods and ingredients or, alternatively, they can be made with close observance to kosher rules. For strict adherents this book assumes that the margarine used in the recipes is always kosher and the following adaptations will be made: Persian

PAREVE FOODS

PAREVE FOODS

PAREVE FOODS

KOSHER WINES

KOSHER MEATS

SOYA MILK & YOGHURT

MATZOHS & BAGELS

Lamb Stew (p.37), substitute the butter with kosher margarine; Mamaliga (p.110), substitute the buttermilk with soya-milk; Sauerbraten (p.139), substitute the white fat with kosher margarine; Turkey Mole (p.186) be sure to use chocolate that is milk-free; Sweet and Sour Meatballs (p.201), be sure to use kosher ginger biscuits; Lemon Cheesecake (p.205), use vegetable gelatin.

Meat and dairy foods, strictly speaking, should not follow directly after each other; there should be an interval. Kosher cooks should therefore adapt some of the menus in this book by substituting butter with kosher margarine, and milk and cream with non-dairy substitutes. You will need to adapt or replace the following: The fetta cheese in Mixed Herb Platter (p.34); Yoghurt with Cucumbers (p.35); the butter in Rice with Fruit (p.35); the butter in Russian Seedcake (p.62); the butter in Brussels Sprouts Viennese (p.136); the butter in Grape Pie (p.187); the condensed milk in Pineapple Flan (p.190); the double cream in Salmon Cakes (p.199); the milk in Cream of Corn Soup (p.201)

To avoid contaminating meat with dairy foods and vice versa, observant households maintain two separate sets of dishes and cooking utensils. Certain foods such as fruits, vegetables, spices, coffee and tea, fish and eggs are considered 'pareve' or neutral. They may be used with meat or milk, although vegetables for a meat meal should be prepared with the meat utensils. The same applies to dairy meals.

The Sabbath and holidays are traditionally ushered in by the *kiddush*, a traditional benediction over wine or bread. Kosher grape wine should be used for the kiddush. A wine is kosher if the grapes have been grown and the wine made by observant Jews.

The interpretation of the kosher laws varies somewhat from country to country and even household to household. The recipes and menus in this book have been written with the practice of the typical modern Jewish cook very much in mind. Many are totally kosher and the few that are not can easily be made so. If you are in doubt about dietary laws any rabbi will be happy to answer your questions.

CHAPTER ONE

Israel

and the Islamic World

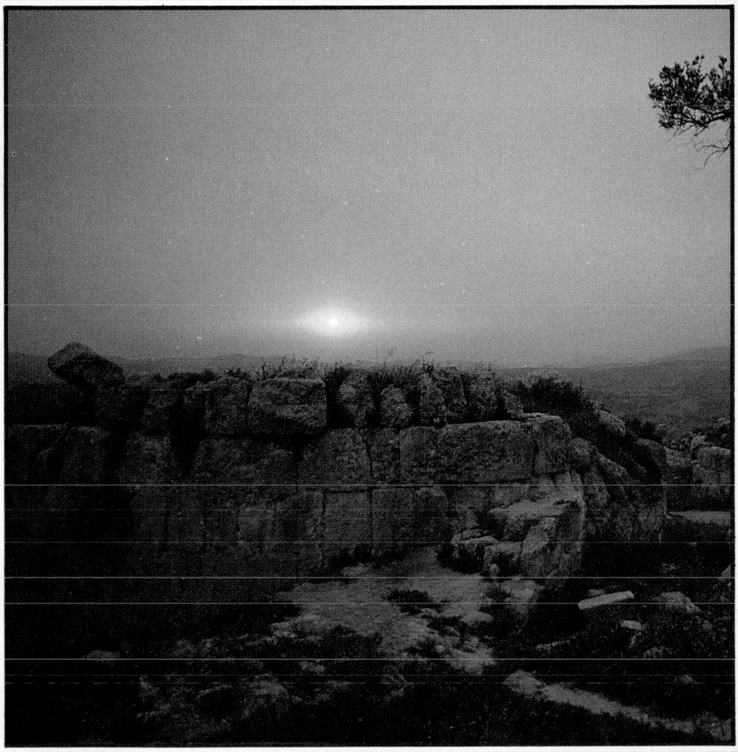

Israel Since the founding of Israel in 1948, Jews from all over the world have come to live there. Many were refugees from Hitler's Europe, but many also came from the oppressed communities of Iran, Iraq, Saudi Arabia, Yemen and North Africa.

Israeli cooking combines elements from both European and Middle Eastern styles, with a strong emphasis on native fruits and vegetables and not very much meat. Many dishes that are widely thought to be Israeli, such as felafel and hummus, in fact originated in Arab countries.

The Middle East The earliest Jewish cuisine originated in the Middle East. Both Islamic and Jewish law forbid the consumption of pork, and Muslims and Jews tend to have a similar diet. The Middle Eastern style of cooking is largely vegetarian and dairy, and uses a lot of herbs and spices. A dish is considered successful if it has a sharp and pronounced contrast of flavours. Among the most popular spices are coriander, turmeric and cardamom. Chicken and lamb are virtually the only meats used. Other important dishes are lentils, bread and couscous.

North Africa Jewish trading communities flourished all along the North African coast from the fifth century BCE to the period of the Islamic conquests in the eighth century CE. During Roman times, as many as six million Jews lived in this thriving area, including nearly a million Jews in Alexandria alone. Their numbers dwindled after Muslim rule was imposed, but were boosted by an influx of Spanish and Portuguese Jews fleeing the Inquisition in the fifteenth century. The Jews of Libya, Algeria, Egypt, Tunisia and Morocco were subject to continuous persecution in the centuries that followed. The Egyptian community, although diminished in size, remained important. The Jews elsewhere in North Africa gradually became trapped in impoverished ghettos.

After 1948, emigration to Israel from North Africa was massive. Fewer than one thousand Jews today remain in Egypt. Of the thirty thousand Jews who lived in Libya before World War II, virtually none remain. The populations of Morocco and Tunisia today are a tenth of their size in 1960.

The North African Jews have a distinct culture. The Tunisian Jews, for example, speak Arabic and have their own rituals. In modern-day Israel, the North African Jews have been largely assimilated, but still maintain many of their unique characteristics.

The religious, ritual and culinary aspects of Jewish life are richly interwoven.

Honey Cake ABOVE *is a classic Jewish dessert*
served around the world (page 20).

♦

Tomato Salad with Olives BELOW *adds a Middle*
Eastern flavour to any main course (page 24).

Baked Perch ABOVE *is a delightfully simple main course for a dairy meal (page 27).*

◆

Lamb and Okra Stew BELOW *is a classic dish of Egyptian-Jewish cuisine (page 31).*

Couscous, a staple dish throughout North Africa,
makes an interesting alternative to rice or pasta
(page 31).

Israeli Dairy Lunch

Israel is a melting pot for Jews from many nations. In that sense, there really is little in the way of native Israeli cuisine. However, the Israelis have made the desert bloom, and the use of fresh fruits and vegetables is characteristic of their cooking.

Melon Grenadine
Sinai Jellied Fish
Courgette Soufflé
Stuffed Pears
Honey Cake

♦

Melon Grenadine

SERVES 6

This delicious starter takes an ordinary melon and turns it into something special.

3 oranges, peeled, seeded and sectioned

1 large pink grapefruit, peeled, seeded and sectioned

6 tbsp Triple Sec or other orange-flavoured liqueur

3 tbsp grenadine syrup

seeds of 1 pomegranate

3 tsp finely chopped fresh mint

3 small Ogen melons, halved and seeded

In a small mixing bowl, combine the orange and grapefruit sections, Triple Sec, grenadine syrup, pomegranate seeds and mint. Refrigerate for 1 hour.
♦ Spoon the fruit mixture evenly into the melon halves.

Sinai Jellied Fish

SERVES 6

This cold fish dish is of Eastern European ancestry. Any firm white fish fillets may be used.

900 g/2 lb fish heads and trimmings

450 ml/$\frac{3}{4}$ pt water

225 ml/8 fl oz white wine

1 celery stalk, diced

1 bay leaf

2 tbsp coarsely chopped parsley

2 onions, quartered

$\frac{1}{2}$ tsp black pepper

2 tbsp lemon juice

$\frac{1}{4}$ tsp salt

2 tbsp olive oil

900 g/2 lb fish fillets

Place all the ingredients except the fish fillets in a medium-sized saucepan. Bring the liquid to a boil over a high heat. Reduce the heat to medium, cover, and cook for 1 hour.
♦ Strain the fish stock through a fine sieve into another saucepan. Discard any solids remaining in the sieve. Add the fish fillets to the fish stock, cover, and simmer over a low heat for 20 minutes.
♦ Carefully remove the fish fillets and place them in a deep dish. Pour the stock over the fish and chill until the stock jellies. Serve cold.

Courgette Soufflé

SERVES 6

French flair combines with a Middle Eastern influence to create this unusual and delicious soufflé.

50 g/2 oz butter

80 g/3 oz finely chopped onion

25 g/1 oz flour

225 ml/8 fl oz milk

1 tbsp grated Parmesan cheese

50 g/2 oz feta cheese, crumbled

450 g/1 lb courgettes, finely chopped

$\frac{1}{4}$ tsp salt

$\frac{1}{4}$ tsp black pepper

4 egg yolks

5 egg whites

Preheat the oven to 180°C/350°F/Gas 4. Melt the butter in a large saucepan over a medium heat. Add the onion and fry for 2 minutes. Add the flour and cook for an additional 2 minutes.

♦ Add the milk and cook, stirring constantly, until the milk begins to bubble and thicken. Add the Parmesan and feta cheese and stir until well mixed.

♦ Add the courgettes, salt and pepper. Reduce the heat to low and cook for 1 minute.

♦ Stir in the egg yolks one at a time. When all the egg yolks are blended, remove the saucepan from the heat.

♦ In a small mixing bowl, beat the egg whites until they are stiff. Fold the egg whites into the courgette soufflé mixture. Pour the mixture into a buttered soufflé dish. Bake for 45 minutes, or until the soufflé is puffed and browned. Serve at once.

Stuffed Pears

SERVES 6

This recipe uses dates and walnuts to create a simple and delightful dessert.

50 g/2 oz dates, stoned and chopped

50 g/2 oz ground walnuts

$\frac{1}{2}$ tsp cinnamon

12 tinned pear halves, drained

125 ml/4 fl oz water

125 g/4 oz sugar

225 ml/8 fl oz white wine

2 whole cloves

2 tbsp lemon juice

Preheat the oven to 180°C/350°F/Gas 4. In a small mixing bowl, combine the dates, walnuts and cinnamon. Mix well. Fill the cavities of the pear halves with the mixture. Place the pears in a shallow baking dish.

♦ In a small saucepan, bring the water, sugar, wine, cloves and lemon juice to a boil over a medium heat. Stir frequently until the sugar is dissolved. Reduce the heat to low and simmer for 2 minutes.

♦ Pour the wine sauce over the pears in the baking dish. Bake for 20 minutes. Chill for 1 hour before serving.

Honey Cake

SERVES 6—8

A classic Jewish dessert all over the world, honey cake is traditionally served on the Sabbath and festivals. In Israel, it is served all year round.

4 tbsp plus 1 tsp vegetable oil
250 g/9 oz flour
4 tbsp sultanas
4 tbsp chopped crystallized orange peel
3 eggs, separated
225 ml/8 fl oz honey
50 g/2 oz sugar
2 tsp finely grated lemon rind
4 tsp instant coffee dissolved in $1\frac{1}{2}$ tbsp boiling water
1 tsp baking powder
$\frac{1}{4}$ tsp bicarbonate of soda
$\frac{1}{4}$ tsp vanilla essence
$\frac{1}{4}$ tsp cinnamon
$\frac{1}{4}$ tsp allspice
$\frac{1}{4}$ tsp salt
50 g/2 oz blanched almonds, sliced

Preheat the oven to 170°C/325°F/Gas 3. Coat a 23×12×7 cm/9×5×3 in baking tin with the teaspoon of vegetable oil. Dust the pan lightly with $1\frac{1}{2}$ tablespoons flour and set aside.

♦ Combine the sultanas, crystallized orange peel, and 2 tablespoons flour in a small mixing bowl. Mix together until the fruit is evenly coated with the flour and set aside.

♦ In another mixing bowl, beat the egg yolks until they begin to froth. Beat in the remaining oil, honey, sugar, lemon rind and concentrated coffee mixture. Gradually beat in the remaining flour, baking powder, bicarbonate of soda, vanilla essence, cinnamon, allspice and salt. Continue beating until the mixture is smooth. Stir in the sultanas and orange peel.

♦ In a small mixing bowl, beat the egg whites until they are stiff. Gently fold the egg whites into the batter. Pour the batter into the greased baking pan and top with the almonds. Bake for 1 hour and 15 minutes. Cool at room temperature.

Israeli Sabbath Meal

This Sabbath meal is an exotic departure from the traditional fare of Jews whose roots are in German-speaking countries and Eastern Europe. Challah would be served with the meal.

Stuffed Dates
Pickled Lemons
Avocado Soup
Chicken with Kumquats
Tomato Salad with Olives
Orange Pudding

Stuffed Dates

SERVES 6—8

This dish of stuffed dates on minced veal cakes should be served with pickled lemons (see below).

15 g/½ oz margarine
450 g/1 lb minced veal
¼ tsp thyme
4 tbsp melted margarine
32 unsalted roasted almonds
32 dried dates, stoned

Melt the margarine in a small frying pan. Add the veal and thyme and cook over a low heat for 15 minutes, or until the veal is thoroughly browned. Drain off any fat that has accumulated in the frying pan. Set the veal aside.

♦ Preheat the oven to 190°C/375°F/Gas 5. When the veal is cool enough to handle, form it into 32 thin meat cakes each with a diameter of about 2.5 cm/1 in. Place the rounds on a greased baking sheet.

♦ Insert an almond into each date. Top each veal round with a stuffed date. Pour the melted margarine over the rounds and bake for 10 minutes. Serve hot.

Pickled Lemons

MAKES 950 ML-1.4 L/32-48 FL OZ

Israel is famous for citrus fruits. Make these lemon pickles three weeks in advance.

12 lemons, thinly sliced and seeded
4 tbsp salt
3 tsp paprika
1 tsp black peppercorns
2 bay leaves
350 ml/12 fl oz corn oil
125 ml/4 fl oz olive oil

Arrange the lemon slices in layers in a colander, sprinkling the salt between the layers. Leave them to stand for 24 hours.

♦ Place the lemon slices in a mixing bowl and sprinkle them with the paprika. Divide the lemon slices between two 450 ml/¾ pt sterilized glass jars. Add ½ teaspoon of the peppercorns and 1 bay leaf to each jar.

♦ Mix the oils together in a bowl. Fill each jar with the oil mixture, making sure that no air bubbles are trapped in the jars. Seal the jars tightly and store them in the refrigerator for 3 weeks before serving.

Avocado Soup

SERVES 6

Similar to pea soup in texture, avocado soup has a delightful nutty flavour.

50 g/2 oz margarine

175 g/6 oz finely chopped onion

3 tbsp flour

1 L/2 pt chicken stock

2 ripe avocados

2 egg yolks

2 tbsp lemon juice

$\frac{1}{2}$ tsp salt

$\frac{1}{2}$ tsp white pepper

Melt the margarine in a small saucepan over a low heat. Add the onions and fry for 2 minutes. Sprinkle the onions with the flour and fry for 3 to 5 minutes longer. Add 225 ml/8 fl oz of the chicken stock and bring the mixture to a boil, stirring frequently.

♦ Pour the onion and stock mixture into a large saucepan. Add the remaining stock and bring the mixture to a boil over a medium heat, stirring frequently. Reduce the heat to very low and simmer, covered, for 5 minutes.

♦ Halve the avocados and remove the stones. Peel the avocado halves and mash the flesh in a bowl. Add the egg yolks, lemon juice, salt and pepper to the bowl and blend well.

♦ Stir the avocado mixture into the soup and cook gently for 3 to 5 minutes. Do not let the soup boil. Serve hot.

Chicken with Kumquats

SERVES 6

This chicken dish has a definite Middle Eastern tang.

2×1.4 kg/3 lb chickens, cut into pieces

450 ml/$\frac{3}{4}$ pt orange juice

4 tbsp apricot preserves

4 tbsp peach preserves

4 tbsp honey

1 tsp cayenne pepper

4 tbsp lemon juice

400 g/14 oz tin kumquats, drained

Preheat the oven to 200°C/400°F/Gas 6. Arrange the chicken pieces in a large, lightly greased baking dish and bake for 30 minutes.

♦ Combine the orange juice, apricot preserves, peach preserves, honey, cayenne pepper and lemon juice in a mixing bowl. Mix well.

♦ After the chicken has baked for 30 minutes, brush the pieces with half the orange juice mixture. Reduce the oven temperature to 180°C/350°F/Gas 4 and bake for 15 minutes.

♦ Turn the chicken pieces over and brush them with the remaining orange juice mixture. Arrange the kumquats in the pan with the chicken. Bake for 15 minutes longer. Pour the pan juices over the chicken and kumquats before serving.

Tomato Salad with Olives

SERVES 6

A crispy contrast to chicken with kumquats (see p.23), this salad is best when made with imported Middle Eastern-style olives.

4 large ripe tomatoes, thinly sliced

2 cucumbers, peeled and thinly sliced

125 g/4 oz black olives, stoned

For the dressing:

2 tbsp finely chopped parsley

1 tbsp finely chopped mint

60 ml/2 fl oz lemon juice

2 tbsp tarragon vinegar

60 ml/2 fl oz olive oil

$\frac{1}{4}$ tsp salt

$\frac{1}{2}$ tsp black pepper

Arrange the tomato and cucumber slices on a serving plate. Arrange the olives around the cucumbers and tomatoes.

♦ To make the dressing, combine the parsley, mint, lemon juice, vinegar, oil, salt and pepper in a small bowl. Mix well with a fork or small whisk until well blended. Pour the dressing over the salad. Chill for 30 minutes and serve cold.

Orange Pudding

SERVES 6

A welcome change from the usual pudding flavours, this recipe has the added advantage of being pareve.

rind from 2 oranges, finely grated

225 g/8 oz sugar

50 g/2 oz cornflour

$\frac{1}{4}$ tsp salt

4 eggs, separated

$1\frac{1}{2}$ pt orange juice

In a large mixing bowl combine the orange rind, sugar, cornflour and salt.

♦ In a separate bowl beat the egg yolks into the orange juice. Gradually add the cornflour mixture and stir until smooth.

♦ Put the mixture into a medium-sized saucepan. Cook over a medium heat, stirring constantly, until the custard mixture thickens, about 12 minutes.

♦ Remove the saucepan from the heat and plunge it into a large pan of cold water. Leave it for 2 to 3 minutes.

♦ Beat the egg whites in a small mixing bowl until they are stiff. Fold the egg whites into the custard until the mixture is smooth. Spoon the pudding into tulip glasses or dessert bowls and chill before serving.

Israeli Dairy Lunch

This traditional dairy lunch includes a baked perch dish that is hundreds of years old.

Fruit Soup
Avocado with Honey Sauce
Baked Perch
Horseradish Condiment
Braised Carrots and Oranges
Almond Loaf

❖

Fruit Soup

SERVES 6

This fruit soup can be made with nearly any fruit in season. It was probably brought to Israel by Jews from Slavic countries.

2 ripe peaches, halved and stoned
4 ripe plums, halved and stoned
3 ripe apricots, halved and stoned
2 apples, peeled, cored and halved
225 g/8 oz strawberries
125 g/4 oz ripe cherries, stoned
60 ml/2 fl oz lemon juice
900 ml/1½ pt water
125 g/4 oz sugar
225 ml/8 fl oz white wine
350 ml/12 fl oz soured cream

Place the fruits, lemon juice, water and sugar in a large pot. Simmer, covered, over a medium heat for 25 minutes.
♦ Turn the heat off. Mash the fruits with a fork into a thick purée. Add the wine. Simmer over a low heat for 5 minutes.
♦ Serve cold, adding a dollop of soured cream to each bowl of soup just before serving.

Avocado with Honey Sauce

SERVES 6—8

The sweetness of the honey, the naturally nutty flavour of the avocado and the citrus tang of the grapefruit make this an interesting starter.

1 onion, finely chopped
1 tsp dry mustard
125 ml/4 fl oz honey
125 ml/4 fl oz lemon juice
125 ml/4 fl oz olive oil
4 large avocados
1 large grapefruit, peeled, seeded and sectioned

In a large mixing bowl, combine the onion, mustard, honey, lemon juice and olive oil. Mix thoroughly. Chill the honey sauce for 30 minutes.
♦ Halve the avocados and remove the stones. Cut each avocado half into wedges approximately the same size as the grapefruit sections. Remove the outer skin. Arrange the avocado wedges alternately with grapefruit sections in small dishes. Spoon some of the honey sauce over each portion and serve.

Baked Perch

SERVES 6—8

This recipe is traditionally made with mushat, a fish native to the Sea of Galilee.
Perch is a good substitute.

8 large perch fillets

$\frac{1}{4}$ tsp salt

$\frac{1}{4}$ tsp black pepper

150 g/5 oz coarsely chopped onion

3 tbsp coarsely chopped parsley

125 ml/4 fl oz white wine

60 ml/2 fl oz lemon juice

60 ml/2 fl oz olive oil

Preheat the oven to 190°C/375°F/Gas 5. In a large baking pan, arrange the perch fillets skin-side down. Sprinkle with the salt and pepper and top with the onion.
♦ Combine the parsley, wine, lemon juice and olive oil in a small mixing bowl. Mix thoroughly.
♦ Pour half the olive oil mixture over the fish and bake for 10 minutes. Baste the fish with the remaining olive oil mixture and bake for 10 minutes longer. Serve immediately.

Horseradish Condiment

MAKES 375 ML/12 FL OZ

3 beetroots, peeled

8 tbsp finely grated fresh white horseradish

$\frac{1}{4}$ tsp black pepper

$2\frac{1}{2}$ tbsp sugar

125 ml/4 fl oz wine vinegar

Cook the beetroots in a large, covered pot of boiling water over a medium heat for 40 minutes. Drain well and chill the beetroots for 30 minutes.
♦ Finely grate or chop the beetroots.
♦ Combine the horseradish, grated beetroot, pepper, sugar and vinegar in a mixing bowl. Mix thoroughly until well blended. Chill and serve with hot or cold fish.

Braised Carrots and Oranges

SERVES 6—8

This side dish goes very well with fish and chicken dishes.

900 g/2 lb baby carrots, scraped
150 g/5 oz onion, chopped
60 ml/ 2 fl oz olive oil
225 ml/8 fl oz water
2 tbsp sugar
2 tsp lemon juice
$\frac{1}{4}$ tsp salt
$\frac{1}{4}$ tsp black pepper
350 g/12 oz tinned mandarin orange sections
60 ml/2 fl oz orange juice

Combine all the ingredients in a medium-sized saucepan. Simmer, uncovered, over a low heat for 15 minutes, stirring frequently. Cover the saucepan and simmer for an additional 5 to 10 minutes, or until the carrots are tender. Serve warm.

Almond Loaf

MAKES 1 LOAF

A deliciously light dessert, almond loaf is also wonderful with morning coffee or afternoon tea.

4 eggs
225 g/8 oz sugar
$\frac{1}{4}$ tsp almond essence
1 tsp baking powder
$\frac{1}{4}$ tsp salt
$\frac{1}{2}$ tsp ground cinnamon
125 g/4 oz flour
15 g/$\frac{1}{2}$ oz melted margarine
175 g/6 oz unsalted, roasted almonds, finely chopped

Preheat the oven to 180°C/350°F/Gas 4. Lightly grease a 23 cm/9 in loaf tin.
♦ Beat the eggs in a mixing bowl. Gradually beat in the sugar. Add the almond essence, baking powder, salt and cinnamon. Add the flour, melted margarine and almonds. Stir until the batter is well blended. Pour the batter into the loaf tin and bake for 40 minutes.
♦ Invert the pan over a cooling rack and turn the loaf out. Let the almond loaf cool. When it is cool, cut it into quarters. Cut the quarters into 1 cm/$\frac{1}{2}$ in slices. Re-form the slices into a loaf shape in the tin and bake at 170°C/325°F/Gas 3 for 10 minutes. Turn off the heat and leave the loaf in the oven for 15 minutes.

Egyptian Jewish Supper

There have been Jews in Egypt for over five thousand years, since long before the pyramids were built. Egyptian-Jewish cuisine developed over the centuries from a means of sustenance into a sophisticated art. It bears some close resemblances to its Muslim and Coptic Christian counterparts.

Bean Cakes
Garlic Sauce
Lamb and Okra Stew
Couscous
Mazza
Semolina Cake

Bean Cakes

SERVES 6

Egyptian cuisine makes great use of beans and vegetables. Serve these bean cakes with garlic sauce (see below). These cakes can be served as a meal on their own, accompanied by salad, rice and pitta bread.

700 g/$1\frac{1}{2}$ lb dried broad beans
225 g/8 oz finely chopped onions
8 tbsp finely chopped parsley
2 tbsp finely chopped fresh coriander
5 garlic cloves, finely chopped
1 tsp salt
$\frac{1}{4}$ tsp black pepper
$\frac{1}{4}$ tsp cayenne pepper
$\frac{1}{2}$ tsp bicarbonate of soda
3 tsp sesame seeds
450 ml/$\frac{3}{4}$ pt vegetable oil

Put the beans into a large bowl and add 2 L/$3\frac{1}{2}$ pt of cold water. Soak the beans for 48 hours, changing the water every 12 hours.

♦ Drain the beans. Squeeze the beans between the fingers to pop off the skins. Discard the skins.

♦ In a large mixing bowl, mash the beans with the onions, parsley, coriander, garlic, salt, black pepper, cayenne pepper and bicarbonate of soda. Mash until smooth.

♦ Shape the bean mixture into small, round cakes about 2.5 cm/1 in in diameter. Sprinkle sesame seeds over both sides of each cake, gently pressing the seeds into the cakes.

♦ Heat the vegetable oil in a large, heavy frying pan over a medium heat until it is very hot. Add as many bean cakes as will fit in a single layer. Cook the cakes for 3 minutes on each side.

Garlic Sauce

MAKES 125 ML/4 FL OZ

Serve the garlic sauce in a small dish with the bean cakes. This garlic sauce also goes well with roast lamb or baked fish.

6 garlic cloves, finely chopped
$\frac{1}{4}$ tsp salt
50 g/2 oz clarified margarine or butter
1 tsp ground coriander
$\frac{1}{4}$ tsp cayenne pepper

Combine all the ingredients in a small saucepan and cook for 2 minutes over a low heat.

Lamb and Okra Stew

SERVES 6

The okra in this stew gives it a natural thickness and savoury taste. Be careful not to overcook the okra, or it will become stringy. Serve the stew with couscous (see below).

3 tbsp margarine

1.1 kg/2½ lb boneless stewing lamb, cubed

150 g/5 oz chopped onion

1 tsp ground cumin

175 g/4 oz tinned tomatoes

4 tbsp tomato purée

125 ml/4 fl oz chicken stock

½ tsp salt

½ tsp black pepper

½ tsp sugar

450 g/1 lb fresh okra

125 g/4 fl oz water

125 g/4 fl oz white vinegar

Melt 2 tablespoons of the margarine in a large frying pan. Add the lamb cubes and fry until they are browned on all sides. Add the onion, cumin, tomatoes, tomato purée, chicken stock, salt, pepper and sugar to the pan. Cook over a low heat, stirring frequently, for 5 minutes.

♦ Preheat the oven to 170°C/325°F/Gas 3. Transfer the lamb mixture from the pan to a medium-sized casserole. Cover the dish and bake for 90 minutes.

♦ Trim the okra and cut it into thin slices. Soak the slices in the water and vinegar for 20 minutes. Drain and pat the okra dry with kitchen paper.

♦ Melt the remaining margarine in a small frying pan. Add the okra slices and fry for 6 minutes, stirring frequently.

♦ After the casserole has baked for 90 minutes, add the okra slices to it. Stir well, cover the dish, and bake for a further 40 minutes. Serve hot.

Couscous

SERVES 6

Couscous is made from a fine wheat semolina. It is a staple dish throughout all of North Africa. Ideally, couscous should be steamed in a large copper couscousier or prepared as described here.

450g/1 lb couscous

225 ml/8 fl oz cold water

125 g/4 oz flour

1 tsp salt

Place the couscous on a large flat plate and shape it into a mound with an indentation in the centre. Fill the indentation with 225 g/8 fl oz water. Using fingers, gradually work the water through the couscous, moistening it evenly.

♦ Mix the flour with the salt in a bowl. Gradually sprinkle the flour mixture over the couscous, working it in until all the grains are coated with flour.

♦ Press the floured grains through a medium sieve. Put the couscous in a metal colander lined with muslin. Place the colander in a pot large enough to hold it. Add enough water to the pot to cover the base or legs of the colander. Cover the pot tightly and steam the couscous for 12 minutes. Break up any lumps with your fingers.

Mazza

SERVES 6

One translation of 'mazza' might be tahini salad, but it is not a salad in the conventional sense of the word. Mazza should be served in small bowls with the main course. It is eaten in small mouthfuls to cleanse the palate. Tahini or sesame seed paste is available in Middle Eastern and well-stocked supermarkets.

2 garlic cloves, finely chopped

$\frac{1}{4}$ tsp salt

175 ml/6 fl oz tahini or sesame seed paste

1 tbsp white wine vinegar

3 tbsp lemon juice

125 ml/4 fl oz water

$\frac{1}{2}$ tsp ground cumin

8 tbsp chopped parsley

$\frac{1}{2}$ head of lettuce, finely chopped

Place all the ingredients in a medium-sized mixing bowl. Stir vigorously until the ingredients are blended and the consistency of the mixture is even.

Semolina Cake

MAKES 1 CAKE

This cake has a delicate sweet flavour. It will keep for weeks if refrigerated. Fine semolina can be purchased at Middle Eastern supermarkets.

125 g/4 oz unsalted margarine, softened

650 g/1 lb 6 oz sugar

1 tsp vanilla essence

2 eggs

450 g/1 lb fine semolina

1 tsp baking powder

$\frac{1}{2}$ tsp bicarbonate of soda

2 tbsp lemon juice

Preheat the oven to 180°C/350°F/Gas 4. Grease a 23×30 cm/9×12 in baking tin.
♦ Combine the margarine, 175 g/6 oz of the sugar, vanilla essence and eggs in a bowl. Blend with a fork until the mixture is light and creamy.
♦ Fold the semolina, baking powder and bicarbonate of soda into the egg mixture. Mix well. Spread the batter in the baking tin. Bake for 35 minutes. Remove the tin from the oven and cool on a rack.
♦ While the cake cools, combine the remaining sugar with water and the lemon juice in a small saucepan. Slowly melt the sugar over a medium heat and bring the mixture to a boil. Cook for 10 minutes. Remove the saucepan from the heat and let the syrup cool until it is only hand-hot. Spoon the syrup over the top of the cake. Cut the cake into small squares and serve.

Iranian Jewish Dinner

Iranian cooking is a cuisine of savoury and contrasting flavours.

Mixed Herb Platter

Kukuye

Yoghurt with Cucumbers

Rice with Fruit

Lentil Dumplings

Peach Pickles

Persian Lamb Stew

Quince Sorbet

Rice Flour Dessert

◆

Mixed Herb Platter

SERVES 6

This delightful dish of fresh herbs and feta cheese is the traditional Iranian way to begin a meal. Serve the herbs with pitta bread.

1 medium-sized bunch flat-leaved parsley

1 small bunch mint sprigs

1 small bunch spring onions

80 g/3 oz fresh chives

1 small bunch fresh tarragon

1 small bunch coriander leaves

1 small bunch watercress

2 small heads of chicory

225 g/½ lb feta cheese, broken into small pieces

Arrange the herbs and cheese on a large dish, preferably silver or pewter.

Kukuye

SERVES 6

The Iranians are very fond of Kukuye, their own special version of omelette. This version uses courgettes.

12 eggs

1 large onion, finely chopped

8 courgettes, thinly sliced

1½ tsp ground turmeric

½ tsp salt

½ tsp black pepper

1 tsp sugar

50 g/2 oz clarified butter

Beat the eggs in a mixing bowl. Add the onion, courgettes, turmeric, salt, pepper and sugar. Mix well.

♦ In a large frying pan, heat the clarified butter over a low heat until it is very hot. Add the egg mixture, cover, and cook for 5 to 7 minutes. If the omelette is entirely solid, remove it from the pan and serve. If the omelette is still semi-solid, replace the lid and cook for a further 2 minutes.

Yoghurt with Cucumbers

SERVES 6

Yoghurt is usually served sweet with added sugar, fruit or preserves in the West. In Iran, yoghurt is used mainly in savoury dishes. Serve this dish along with the Mixed Herb Platter and pitta bread.

750 ml/$1\frac{1}{4}$ pt unflavoured yoghurt

2 large cucumbers, peeled, thickly sliced and then quartered

2 large onions, finely chopped

50 g/2 oz walnuts, chopped

$\frac{1}{2}$ tsp salt

$\frac{1}{2}$ tsp white pepper

2 tbsp chopped fresh mint

Combine all the ingredients in a large mixing bowl, and mix thoroughly, taking care not to bruise the cucumber slices.

Rice with Fruit

SERVES 6

Rice is the principal staple food of Iran. This is Iran's most celebrated rice dish.

50 g/2 oz clarified butter

1 onion, finely chopped

450 g/1 lb plaice fillets, cut into small pieces

$\frac{1}{2}$ tsp ground cinnamon

350 g/12 oz fresh or tinned sour cherries, stoned

50 g/2 oz unsalted almonds, chopped

150 g/5 oz currants, or raisins

70 g/$2\frac{1}{2}$ oz dried apricots

$1\frac{1}{2}$ tsp salt

$\frac{1}{2}$ tsp black pepper

500 g/1 lb long grain rice, rinsed and drained

1 L/2 pt water

Heat the butter in a large frying pan. Add the onion and plaice pieces and fry over a low heat for 10 minutes. Stir constantly.

♦ Add the cinnamon, cherries, almonds, currants, apricots, salt and pepper to the pan. Stir and simmer for 3 to 4 minutes.

♦ Add the rice and water. Stir gently but well. Cover tightly and simmer over a very low heat for 55 minutes.

Lentil Dumplings

SERVES 6

Dough and lentil combinations are a protein staple of the Middle East with no real equivalent in Western cuisine. These vegetarian dumplings are filling and highly nutritious.

350 g/12 oz brown lentils

750 ml/1¼ pt cold water

225 ml/8 fl oz lukewarm water

1 tbsp grenadine syrup

1 packet active dry yeast

400 g/14 oz flour

1½ tsp salt

½ tsp ground cardamom

175 g/6 oz clarified butter

2 large onions, finely chopped

2 tbsp brown sugar

950 ml/32 fl oz vegetable oil

Place the lentils in a large pot and add 750 ml/1¼ pt cold water. Cover the pot and bring the liquid to a boil over a medium heat. Cook the lentils until the water has been absorbed and the lentils are tender, about 1 hour 15 minutes.

♦ While the lentils are cooking, make the dough. Pour the lukewarm water into a bowl and stir in the grenadine syrup. Add the yeast and stir until it dissolves. Let the mixture stand for 5 minutes.

♦ In a large bowl, combine the flour, 1 teaspoon of salt and cardamom. Add the yeast mixture and 50 g/2 oz of the clarified butter to the flour. Stir to form a soft dough.

♦ Turn the dough out on to a lightly floured surface and knead it with a rolling pin for 10 to 12 minutes. Shape the dough into a ball, put it into a bowl, and leave it to stand in a warm place for 50 minutes.

♦ Punch down the dough and cut it in half with a sharp knife. Roll each half out into a large, flat circle. Cut the dough into 7.5 cm/3 in rounds with a pastry cutter.

♦ When the lentils are done, mash them with a fork to make a smooth purée. Heat the remaining clarified butter in a frying pan and add the onions and lentil purée. Stir in ½ teaspoon of salt and the brown sugar. Cook over a low heat for 5 minutes.

♦ Place a spoonful of the lentil filling into the centre of each dough round. Moisten the edges of the round with water and fold the dumpling over. Press the edges together with the blunt edge of a spoon or knife to seal.

♦ Heat the vegetable oil in a large saucepan over a medium heat until it is very hot. Add the dumplings in batches of 8 and cook each batch for 3 to 5 minutes, or until the dumplings are golden brown. Remove the dumplings with a slotted spoon and drain on kitchen towels. Serve warm.

ISRAEL AND THE ISLAMIC WORLD

Peach Pickles

SERVES 6

This delightful Iranian savoury should be made a week in advance. Tamarind paste is available in Middle Eastern supermarkets.

450 ml/¾ pt white wine vinegar

1½ tbsp grated fresh ginger

3½ tsp ground coriander

4 garlic cloves, finely chopped

2 tsp tamarind paste

225 g/8 oz sugar

½ tsp cayenne pepper

½ tsp salt

¼ tsp black pepper

700 g/1½ lb fresh peaches, peeled, stoned and sliced

Place all the ingredients except the peaches in a large mixing bowl, and stir with a fork until well mixed.

♦ Put the peaches in a large pan. Add the vinegar mixture and bring to a boil over a high heat. Cook for 8 minutes. Pour the peaches and pickling liquid into a large sterilized jar. Leave it to cool. Seal the jar and refrigerate for 1 week before using.

Persian Lamb Stew

SERVES 6—8

Lots of fresh parsley is crucial to this dish. Use the flat-leaved kind for maximum flavour.

6 tbsp butter

2 spring onions, finely chopped

80 g/3 oz finely chopped parsley

1.5 kg/3½ lb lean lamb, cubed

1.75 L/3¼ pt water

90 ml/3 fl oz fresh lemon juice

1 lemon, cut into small wedges

2 450-g/1-lb tins red kidney beans, drained

1 scant tbsp salt

2 tsp freshly ground black pepper

Melt 3 tablespoons of the butter in a large saucepan. Add the spring onions and parsley and fry until the parsley turns a dark green.

♦ Melt the remaining butter in a large frying pan. Add the cubed lamb and fry until the cubes are lightly browned.

♦ Add the lamb to the saucepan. Add the water, lemon juice and lemon wedges. Stir well, cover and simmer for 1 hour 15 minutes. Stir in the kidney beans, salt and pepper. Cover and simmer for another 20 minutes, or until the lamb is tender. Serve with rice.

Quince Sorbet

SERVES 6

This distinctive Middle Eastern sorbet can be served with dairy or meat meals. Serve it in tulip or dessert glasses.

3 large ripe quinces, peeled, cored and cut into small pieces
700 ml/24 fl oz water
700 g/24 oz sugar
60 ml/2 fl oz lemon juice

Put the fruit and water into a large saucepan. Bring the mixture to a boil over a high heat. Reduce the heat to low and simmer for 40 minutes.

♦ Strain the mixture through a sieve into another saucepan. Discard any solids that remain in the sieve. Add the sugar and lemon juice and bring the mixture to a boil over a high heat. Boil for 10 minutes, stirring frequently to dissolve the sugar. Remove the saucepan from the heat and let the mixture cool for 5 minutes.

♦ Pour the sorbet mixture into a large bowl and put it in the ice compartment of the refrigerator or the freezer for 2 hours. Stir the mixture every 10 to 15 minutes to break up the ice crystals and make a smooth texture.

Rice Flour Dessert

SERVES 6—8

The unusual flavour of this dessert comes in part from the rose water. Well-stocked chemists sell rose water. Rice flour can either be bought or made at home by pulverizing rice in a liquidizer or food processor.

3 tbsp sesame oil
3 tbsp vegetable oil
125 g/4 oz rice flour
950 ml/32 fl oz milk
2 tbsp rose water
1 tbsp almond essence
125 g/4 oz sugar
1 tsp ground cardamom
$\frac{1}{8}$ tsp ground cinnamon
125 g/4 oz castor sugar
125 g/4 oz pistachio nuts, chopped

Heat the sesame and vegetable oils together in a saucepan over a moderate heat. Stir in the rice flour and cook until the flour is a light golden brown colour. Reduce the heat to low and stir in the milk. Continue stirring until the milk and flour mixture is smooth. Add the rose water, almond essence, sugar, cardamom and cinnamon. Cook the mixture over a low heat, stirring constantly, until it thickens. Add the castor sugar and stir until it dissolves.

♦ Pour the mixture into a lightly greased long shallow tin, sprinkle the top with the pistachio nuts, and allow it to cool and become firm. Cut into rectangles or squares.

Yemenite Jewish Supper

This unusual menu includes a broad sample of Yemenite cuisine. Some of the recipes, such as the Yemenite Herring and the Banana Cakes, originated with the Yemenite Jews. The others are enjoyed by Jews and Muslims alike. As meat in Yemen is neither cheap nor plentiful, the cuisine makes great use of every part of the animal.

Flatbread
Hilbeh
Zhug
Liver and Kidney Stew
Herring Yemen-Style
Banana Cakes

Flatbread

MAKES 8—10 BREADS

This very simple bread has a lot of flavour. Serve it warm with Hilbeh and Zhug at the beginning of the meal.

350 g/12 oz wholemeal flour
1 tsp salt
225 ml/8 fl oz water
60 ml/2 fl oz vegetable oil

In a large mixing bowl, combine the flour, salt and water. Stir until the consistency of the dough is soft and even throughout. Turn the dough out on to a lightly floured surface and knead for 10 to 12 minutes. Form the dough into a ball. Place the ball in a mixing bowl and cover with clingfilm. Leave it to stand for $2\frac{1}{2}$ hours.
♦ Divide the dough into balls with a diameter of about 4 cm/$1\frac{1}{2}$ in. Roll the balls into small thin circles. Let the dough rounds stand for 25 minutes.
♦ In a large, heavy frying pan heat the oil until it is very hot. Place the dough circles one at a time in the hot oil and cook for 2 minutes each over a moderate heat. Turn the circles over and fry for 1 minute longer.
♦ After each bread circle is cooked, place it in a dish lined with kitchen paper to drain. Keep warm.

Hilbeh

SERVES 6—8

Hilbeh is a dip traditionally eaten with flatbread at the start of a meal. Fenugreek seeds are available in Middle Eastern supermarkets.

3 tsp fenugreek seeds
225 ml/8 fl oz cold water
3 garlic cloves, finely chopped
25 g/1 oz fresh coriander leaves, very finely chopped
$\frac{1}{4}$ tsp salt
$1\frac{1}{2}$ tbsp lemon juice
$\frac{1}{4}$ tsp cayenne pepper

Put the fenugreek seeds into a small bowl and add the cold water. Soak the seeds for 12 hours. Drain well.
♦ In a large wooden mixing bowl, combine the fenugreek seeds with the garlic, coriander, salt, lemon juice and cayenne pepper. Combine thoroughly until the mixture is a smooth purée. Place the mixture in a glass bowl, cover and chill before serving.

Zhug

SERVES 6—8

Zhug is a spicy dip with a markedly different taste from Hilbeh. Serve it chilled.

3 cardamom pods

1 tsp black peppercorns

2 tsp caraway seeds

4 hot chilli peppers, finely chopped

25 g/1 oz coriander leaves, finely chopped

25 g/1 oz watercress, finely chopped

6 garlic cloves, finely chopped

½ tsp salt

60 ml/2 fl oz cold water

Grind the cardamom pods, peppercorns and caraway seeds into a powder using a mortar and pestle. Combine the spice powder with the chillis, coriander, watercress, garlic, salt and water in a bowl. Mix well.

♦ Place the mixture in a small saucepan and bring it to a boil over a moderate heat. Reduce the heat to low and simmer for 10 minutes. Spoon the mixture into a glass jar, cover, and chill.

Liver and Kidney Stew

SERVES 6—8

This delicious stew will tempt even confirmed liver-haters. It is important to follow the soaking directions in order for the liver to be kosher.

900 g/2 lb fresh lamb liver

4 lamb kidneys, skin and core removed

60 ml/2 fl oz vegetable oil

2 large onions, coarsely chopped

5 garlic cloves, finely chopped

1 tsp ground turmeric

350 ml/12 fl oz tomato purée

1½ tsp ground coriander

¾ tsp ground cumin

2 cardamom pods

125 ml/4 fl oz water

1 tbsp coarsely chopped fresh coriander

1 tbsp coarsely chopped parsley

1 tsp salt

½ tsp black pepper

Soak the liver and kidneys in lightly salted cold water for 40 minutes. Drain well and pat dry with kitchen paper. Cut the liver into small cubes, removing any tough membranes and tubes. Cut the kidneys into cubes.

♦ Heat the oil in a large, heavy frying pan. Add the onion, garlic and turmeric and fry over a low heat for 5 minutes. Add the liver and kidney cubes and fry for a further 10 minutes, or until the meat is lightly browned all over.

♦ Add the tomato purée, dried coriander, cumin, cardamom pods, water, fresh coriander, parsley, salt and pepper. Cover and simmer over a low heat for 90 minutes. Check every half hour adding water if necessary. Serve hot.

Herring Yemen-style

SERVES 6—8

Herring Yemen-style was originally prepared over an open fire. This recipe has been adapted for use in modern kitchens.

4 salt herrings, cut into small pieces
4 tbsp coriander leaves chopped
1 tbsp fresh or 1 tsp dried marjoram
$\frac{1}{4}$ tsp salt
$\frac{1}{4}$ tsp black pepper
1 large pimento, finely chopped
1 tbsp chopped parsley
75 g/6 oz finely chopped onion

Place the herring pieces in a large glass or ceramic, not metal, baking dish. Cover the herring with the coriander, marjoram, salt, pepper, pimento, parsley and onion. Cover the dish and marinate in the refrigerator for 6 hours.

♦ Preheat the grill. Remove the herring pieces from the marinade and place them in a flameproof dish. Grill until they are lightly browned, about 15 minutes.

Banana Cakes

SERVES 6—8

The perfect ending to a Middle Eastern meal, these banana cakes have a sweet, nutty flavour.

450 g/1 lb flour
3 tsp sugar
$1\frac{1}{2}$ tsp salt
4 tbsp margarine
4 bananas, mashed to a paste
125-225 ml/4-8 fl oz water
175 ml/6 fl oz vegetable oil

Combine the flour, sugar, salt, margarine and mashed bananas in a large mixing bowl. Mix well. Add enough of the water to stiffen the dough. Cover the bowl and leave it to stand for 25 minutes.

♦ Turn the dough out on to a lightly floured surface. Roll the dough out into a thin sheet. Cut the dough into 10 cm/4 in squares.

♦ In a large, heavy frying pan, heat the oil until it is very hot. Fry the dough squares, one at a time until they are golden brown, about 3 minutes for the first side and 2 minutes for the second. Serve warm.

Syrian Lebanese Dinner

Modern Israeli cooking is strongly influenced by the cuisine of the Jews of Lebanon and Syria. Felafel, for example, which is assumed by many to be an Israeli invention, is in fact an age-old creation of the Syrian-Lebanese Jews.

Chard Soup with Lentils
Stuffed Artichokes
Felafel
Lebanese Cauliflower
Potato Salad
Nut Pudding

◆

Chard Soup with Lentils

SERVES 6—8

Yet another version of Middle Eastern lentil soup. Kale or fresh spinach may be. substituted for the chard.

450 g/1 lb dried brown lentils

1.75 L/3¼ pt water

60 ml/2 fl oz olive oil

2 large onions, finely chopped

6 garlic cloves, coarsely chopped

50 g/2 oz torn Swiss chard leaves, tough stems removed

4 tbsp chopped coriander

½ tsp salt

¼ tsp black pepper

60 ml/2 fl oz lemon juice

Pick over the lentils and wash them. Put the lentils into a large saucepan and add the water. Cover and cook over a medium heat for 1 hour.

♦ When the lentils have cooked for 50 minutes, heat the olive oil in a frying pan over a low heat. Add the onions, garlic and chard and fry for 8 minutes, stirring constantly.

♦ Add the chard mixture to the lentils. Add the coriander, salt, pepper and lemon juice and stir well. Cover the saucepan and simmer over a low heat for 20 minutes. Serve hot.

Stuffed Artichokes

SERVES 8

Lamb is the principal meat served in Lebanon and Syria.

1 tbsp olive oil

1 onion, finely chopped

4 tbsp pine kernels

450 g/1 lb ground lamb

2 tbsp chopped parsley

½ tsp black pepper

¼ tsp salt

8 large artichokes, stems trimmed and outermost leaves removed

900 ml/1½ pt water

2 tbsp margarine

60 ml/2 fl oz lemon juice

Heat the oil in a small saucepan. Add the onion and pine kernels and cook for 3 to 5 minutes over a low heat.

♦ Combine the ground lamb with the onions and pine kernels in a small mixing bowl. Add the parsley, pepper and salt. Mix thoroughly.

♦ Stuff the artichokes with the meat mixture, inserting small quantities between the leaves with a teaspoon.

♦ Place the artichokes upright in 2 large saucepans, 4 in each pan. Fill each pan with 450 ml/¾ pt water. Reduce the heat to low and cover the pots. Steam the artichokes for 45 minutes and then drain well.

♦ In a small saucepan, melt the margarine and add in the lemon juice. Pour the mixture over the artichokes and simmer for 15 minutes. Serve warm.

Felafel

SERVES 8

If you are serving felafel with a meat meal, be sure to use only tahini sauce and not a yoghurt-tahini mix.

225 g/8 oz dried fava beans

225 g/8 oz dried chick peas

3 garlic cloves, chopped

1 medium onion, finely chopped

5 tbsp finely chopped parsley

$\frac{1}{4}$ tsp cayenne pepper

1 tsp ground coriander

$\frac{1}{2}$ tsp ground cumin

1 tsp bicarbonate of soda

$\frac{1}{2}$ tsp salt

$\frac{1}{4}$ tsp black pepper

950 ml/32 fl oz vegetable oil

8 pitta breads

$\frac{1}{2}$ head shredded lettuce

175 g/6 oz ripe tomatoes, cubed

125 ml/4 fl oz tahini sauce

Soak the fava beans in 750 ml/1$\frac{1}{4}$ pt cold water for 48 hours.
♦ Soak the chickpeas in 750 ml/1$\frac{1}{4}$ pt cold water for 12 hours.
♦ Drain the fava beans well. Drain the chickpeas well and rub them through a sieve.
♦ Combine the fava beans and sieved chickpeas with the garlic and onion in a large wooden mixing bowl. Chop together until the consistency is even.
♦ Mix in the parsley, cayenne pepper, coriander, cumin, bicarbonate of soda, salt and pepper. Combine thoroughly and stand for 20 minutes.
♦ Shape the mixture into about 30 balls and leave for 30 minutes.
♦ In a medium-sized saucepan heat the oil until it is very hot. Drop in as many felafel balls as will fill the saucepan without crowding. Cook the balls for 6 or 7 minutes. Drain on kitchen paper. Repeat the process with the remaining felafel balls.
♦ Slice the top off each pitta bread and open it up. Place 3 to 4 felafel balls in each pocket with some lettuce and tomato. Top with tahini sauce.

Lebanese Cauliflower

SERVES 6—8

The addition of tahini sauce gives this cauliflower dish an exotic flavour.

1 large cauliflower, trimmed

225 ml/8 fl oz tahini sauce

2 tbsp sesame seeds

$\frac{1}{2}$ tsp lemon juice

$\frac{1}{2}$ tsp paprika

$\frac{1}{2}$ small onion, finely chopped

Place the cauliflower in a medium-sized saucepan and add 450 ml/$\frac{3}{4}$ pt cold water. Cover the pan and steam the cauliflower for 12 to 14 minutes, or until tender.
♦ Combine the tahini, sesame seeds, lemon juice, paprika and onion. Stir well.
♦ Drain the cauliflower and place it on a serving dish and pour the tahini sauce mixture over it while the cauliflower is still hot. Serve hot.

Potato Salad

SERVES 6—8

Mint and lots of parsley give this potato salad a refreshingly different taste.

8 potatoes, unpeeled

1 small onion, finely chopped

6 tbsp finely chopped parsley

1 tsp dried mint or 1 tbsp chopped fresh mint

$\frac{1}{4}$ tsp black pepper

2 garlic cloves, very finely chopped

125 ml/4 fl oz lemon juice

125 ml/4 fl oz olive oil

Cook the potatoes in a large pan of boiling salted water for 10 to 15 minutes, or until they are tender but not mushy.

♦ Drain the potatoes and cut them into chunks. Put the chunks into a large salad bowl.

♦ In a large mixing bowl, combine the onions, parsley, mint, pepper, garlic, lemon juice and olive oil. Mix well. Pour the dressing over the potatoes. Toss well. Serve at room temperature.

Nut Pudding

SERVES 8

This traditional Syrian nut pudding is enjoyed by both Jews and Muslims. Use white, not green, pistachio nuts.

900 ml/$1\frac{1}{2}$ pt single cream or non-dairy cream substitute

125 g/4 oz ground rice

$\frac{1}{4}$ tsp salt

125 g/4 oz sugar

80 g/3 oz ground unsalted almonds

80 g/3 oz ground unsalted pistachio nuts

2 tbsp grenadine syrup

In a medium-sized saucepan, bring the cream to a boil. Add the ground rice, salt and sugar. Simmer over a medium heat for 5 minutes, stirring constantly.

♦ Stir in the ground almonds, ground pistachios and grenadine syrup. Reduce the heat to low and simmer for 2 minutes, stirring constantly.

♦ Remove the saucepan from the heat and let the mixture cool until it is warm. Spoon the pudding into small individual dessert dishes and chill. Serve cold.

Israeli
Middle Eastern Lunch

The Israelis are noted for their abundant breakfasts and lunches, which, perhaps as a result of the warm climate, feature fresh fruits and vegetables and salads. This menu consists of Middle Eastern specialities in that tradition. Pitta bread is eaten throughout the area at every meal. The tarama salad is really Greek in origin, but is commonly served in Israel. Dessert, if there needed to be one, would be fresh fruit. With the possible exception of the spiced fish, any of these dishes could be served for breakfast as well.

Hummus

Spiced Fish

Pitta Bread

Tabouleh

Lentil and Feta Cheese Salad

Tarama Salad

Hummus

SERVES 6—8

This garlicky chickpea dip is a favourite starter in the Middle East. Serve it with pitta bread or crudités.

> 2-450 g/1-lb tins of cooked chickpeas, drained
> 125 ml/4 fl oz tahini (sesame seed paste)
> 1 medium-sized onion, quartered
> 125 ml/4 fl oz fresh lemon juice
> 2 garlic cloves, chopped
> $\frac{1}{2}$ tsp paprika
> $\frac{1}{2}$ tsp dried coriander
> $\frac{1}{2}$ tsp ground cumin
> $\frac{1}{2}$ tsp salt
> $\frac{1}{2}$ tsp freshly ground black pepper
> $1\frac{1}{2}$ tbsp water
> 3 tbsp fresh parsley, coarsely chopped

Put the chickpeas, tahini, onion, lemon juice, garlic, paprika, coriander, cumin, salt, pepper and water into a food processor or liquidizer. Blend until smooth and creamy. Pour the hummus into a serving dish. Garnish with the chopped parsley.

Spiced Fish

SERVES 6

This simple but flavourful way to prepare fish makes an excellent main course for dairy menus.

> 60 ml/2 fl oz lemon juice
> $\frac{1}{2}$ tsp ground ginger
> $\frac{1}{2}$ tsp finely chopped garlic
> $\frac{1}{4}$ tsp ground cumin
> $\frac{1}{2}$ tsp paprika
> $\frac{1}{4}$ tsp cayenne pepper
> $\frac{1}{4}$ tsp ground turmeric
> $\frac{1}{2}$ tsp salt
> 225 ml/8 fl oz white wine
> 1.4 kg/3 lb flounder fillets

Preheat the oven to 190°C/375°F/Gas 5. In a small mixing bowl, combine all the ingredients except the flounder fillets. Mix well.
♦ Arrange the fillets in a large baking dish and pour the sauce over them. Bake for 15 minutes. Serve hot.

Pitta Bread

MAKES 20 SMALL LOAVES

Small round flat loaves of pitta bread are increasingly popular in the West. When cut in half, the loaves form convenient pockets for sandwiches.

40 g/1½ oz dry yeast
1 tsp sugar
275 ml/½ pt warm water
900 g/2 lb flour
1 tsp salt

Preheat the oven to 240°C/475°F/Gas 9.

♦ Put the yeast and sugar in a mixing bowl, add the warm water and stir lightly to dissolve the dry ingredients. Stir in the flour and salt and continue stirring until a dough forms. Knead the dough for 8 to 10 minutes. Divide the dough into 20 balls. Roll out each dough ball to 1 cm/⅜ in thickness. Cover the rolled out circles with a damp cloth and leave to rise for 30 minutes. Roll out the circles again and leave to rise for another 30 minutes.

♦ Put the 20 dough circles on a well-greased baking sheet. Bake the pitta for 3 minutes or until the breads are puffed up and lightly browned. Serve at once or store in a plastic bag to keep moist.

Tabouleh

SERVES 6

Serve tabouleh as a starter with pitta bread. Be sure to use fresh, not dried, mint.

225 g/8 oz burghul wheat
450 ml/¾ pt boiling water
50 g/2 oz chopped spring onion
5 tbsp chopped fresh mint
2 medium-sized tomatoes, seeded and chopped
25 g/1 oz chopped fresh parsley
4 tbsp olive oil
5 tbsp fresh lemon juice
½ tsp salt
½ tsp freshly ground black pepper
10 large lettuce leaves

Put the burghul into a bowl and add the boiling water. Stir, cover the bowl, and leave to stand for 35 minutes.

♦ Drain the burghul, squeezing out any remaining water between the palms of your hands. Put the burghul into a serving bowl. Add the spring onions, mint, tomatoes and parsley. Toss gently. Add the olive oil. Stir until well mixed. Add the lemon juice, salt and pepper. Stir until well mixed.

♦ Serve the tabouleh in the serving bowl or on individual plates. Use the lettuce leaves as scoops to eat the tabouleh.

Lentil and Feta Cheese Salad

SERVES 6

This hearty salad is a meal in itself. Serve it with pitta bread.

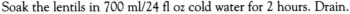

350 g/¾ lb brown lentils
1 bay leaf
½ tsp dried basil
2 garlic cloves, crushed
80 g/3 oz diced celery
1 small onion, chopped
80 g/3 oz crumbled feta cheese
8 tbsp chopped fresh chives
For the dressing:
6 tbsp olive oil
3 tbsp wine vinegar
⅛ tsp dried oregano
½ tsp salt
½ tsp freshly ground black pepper

Soak the lentils in 700 ml/24 fl oz cold water for 2 hours. Drain.
♦ Put the lentils into a saucepan and add enough cold water to cover them completely. Add the bay leaf, basil and one of the garlic cloves. Bring to a boil and then reduce the heat. Simmer, covered, for 20 minutes.
♦ Add the celery and onion. Add enough additional water to cover the lentils. Cover the saucepan and simmer for 10 more minutes.
♦ Drain the lentils. Discard the bay leaf and garlic clove.
♦ Put the lentils into a serving bowl. Add the feta cheese and chives. Toss.
♦ Put the olive oil, vinegar, oregano, remaining garlic clove, salt and pepper into a jar with a tightly fitting lid. Cover tightly and shake until well blended.
♦ Pour the dressing over the lentil salad and toss. Let the salad stand at room temperature for 2 hours, tossing occasionally, before serving.

Tarama Salad

SERVES 6—8

This dip makes a good starter for lunch. Serve it with sliced cucumbers and tomatoes and pitta bread.

3 large potatoes
3 tbsp milk
125 g/4 oz red caviar or red roe
6 tbsp water
60 ml/2 fl oz lemon juice
1 small onion, finely chopped
175 ml/6 fl oz olive oil

Peel the potatoes. Cook them in boiling water until very soft, about 20 minutes.
♦ Drain the potatoes and put them into a mixing bowl. By hand or with an electric mixer, mash the potatoes, slowly adding the milk, until smooth. Add the caviar and water to the potatoes. Mix well. Add the lemon juice and onion to the mixture and mix briefly. Slowly beat in the olive oil. Continue to beat until a smooth paste is formed.

Mixed Herb Platter ABOVE, *a traditional Iranian
Jewish first course, is served here with Yoghurt and
Cucumbers (page 34).*

◆

Rice with Fruit BELOW *is Iran's most celebrated rice
dish (page 35).*

Zhug ABOVE *is a spicy dip from the*
Yemen (page 41).

♦

Banana Cakes BELOW LEFT *make a perfect ending*
to a Middle Eastern meal (page 42).

♦

Felafel BELOW RIGHT *is a traditional Middle Eastern*
dish, served in Pitta Bread (page 45).

*Lebanese Cauliflower topped with Tahini Sauce
makes an exotic vegetable side dish (page 45).*

CHAPTER TWO

Russia

and Eastern Europe

The Khazar Jewish kingdom was a fascinating episode in Russian Jewish history. The Khazars were a pagan, nomadic tribe living in the area between the Black Sea and the Caspian Sea and to the north. Their king converted to Judaism in about 700. In the three centuries that followed, many Khazars became Jews and Jews from elsewhere were invited to settle in the kingdom. The Russians to the north began attacking the kingdom in 970, and in 1016 a combined Russian-Byzantine attack destroyed the kingdom. The Jews dispersed into Russia, Armenia, Byzantium and the Mediterranean coast. It is likely that many of the Jews of these regions are descended from Khazar refugees.

Jews have lived in Russia and the Eastern European countries ever since. In the eleventh and twelfth centuries and again in the fifteenth century many Russians converted to Judaism. The Jews were always under suspicion, however, and in 1804 the Pale of Settlement was established. This forced Jews in Russia, the Ukraine and Poland to live in ghettos and restricted areas. Their economic and educational opportunities were extremely limited. Despite this and despite continuing persecution, the Jews of Eastern Europe developed vital and thriving communities. Even so, millions fled oppression for new lives in America, England and elsewhere. More recently, many Soviet Jews have emigrated to Israel and America.

Because so many of these Jews left their homelands for Western Europe and America, it is their cooking that is often identified as 'Jewish'. Traditional dishes such as cholent, kugel, kasha, blintzes and stuffed cabbage are all part of this cuisine. The Jews of Poland were famous for their herring dishes and developed arguably the definitive version of stuffed cabbage. They also created a huge variety of kugels (baked puddings). The Romanian Jews shared their Gentile counterparts' enjoyment of dishes with a sour flavour. The Romanians were also fine bakers, rivalling the famed pastry empire of Vienna. Hungarian Jews were fond of fruit soups. They also developed their own distinct version of lesco, a traditional Hungarian vegetable dish. All Hungarian cooking, both Jewish and Gentile, relies heavily on exotic seasonings such as nutmeg and paprika. Kohlrabi, a vegetable unusual in Western-style cooking, was also popular. The Jews of Yugoslavia enjoyed vegetable caviar, lamb and the famous dessert preserves called slatko.

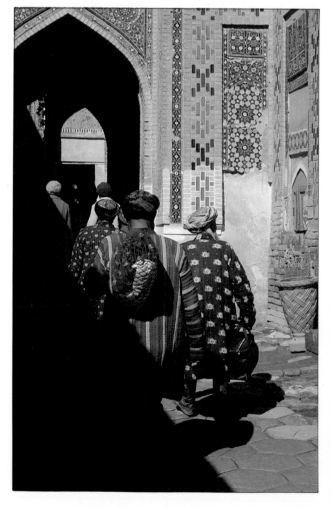

Jews settled all over Russia and Eastern Europe, from Leningrad to Samarkand and Bucharest. Their diverse cultural history is reflected in their cuisine.

Russian Sabbath Dinner

This traditional dinner might have been served on Friday or Saturday
night in a relatively prosperous Jewish household in Moscow at the turn
of the century. It shows traditional Jewish and Russian influences, as
well as the influence of the French. It should be noted that sturgeon
caviar, which was often eaten by the more cosmopolitan Jews of Moscow
and St Petersburg, was not eaten by the more orthodox Jews, who felt
that, as a bottom feeder, the sturgeon was unclean. However, as
sturgeon caviar is not unkosher in the strict sense of the word, it is
included as an authentic part of the meal. Three different drinks were
served with the meal, in addition to the traditional red grape wine used
for the blessing. A white wine or aperitif was served before the meal or
with the starter, red wine was served with the main course, and
flavoured vodka or slivovitz, a potent fruit brandy, was served with
dessert.

Chopped Chicken Livers
New Potatoes with Caviar
Pickled Herring in
Raspberry Vinegar
Stuffed Peppers
Russian Egg Drop Soup
Cholent
Cabbage Salad
Russian Seedcake

Zakuski: Chopped Chicken Livers

SERVES 6—10

A traditional Friday night dinner in a comfortable Russian-Jewish home would start with a zakuski, a variety of different hors d'oeuvres served together. A typical zakuski would consist of four to ten separate dishes. Each person would be served with a little of each zakuski on a traditional enamelled plate.

450 g/1 lb fresh chicken livers
60 ml/2 fl oz mayonnaise
2 hard-boiled eggs
4 tbsp chopped celery
4 tbsp chopped onion
½ tsp salt
½ tsp freshly ground black pepper

Put the chicken livers into a saucepan and cover completely with cold water. Bring to a boil and cook for 10 to 12 minutes. Drain the livers well.

♦ In a large mixing bowl, combine the livers with the mayonnaise and eggs. Mash the mixture with a fork. Add the celery, onion, salt and pepper. Mash until the mixture has an even, fine consistency.

♦ Put the mixture into a serving bowl, cover, and chill for at least 1 hour before serving. Serve with crusty bread, melba toast or biscuits.

Zakuski: New Potatoes with Caviar

SERVES 6—8

6 medium-sized new potatoes
25 g/1 oz black caviar
25 g/1 oz red caviar
8 hard-boiled egg yolks, crumbled
3 lemons, quartered

Cook the potatoes in a large pot of boiling water until they are tender, about 20 to 30 minutes. Drain well.

♦ When the potatoes are cool enough to handle, cut them in half lengthwise. Scoop a small pocket out of each half with a teaspoon.

♦ Fill six of the potato halves with the black caviar; fill the remaining halves with the red caviar. Sprinkle the crumbled egg yolks over each potato. Put both a red and black potato half on each zakuski plate and garnish with lemon wedges.

Zakuski: Pickled Herring

SERVES 6—10

675 g/1½ lb pickled herring (rollmops)

125 ml/4 fl oz raspberry vinegar

70 g/2½ oz small onions, diced

1 tsp freshly ground black pepper

½ tsp tarragon

125 ml/4 fl oz white wine

80 g/3 oz cooked peas

Drain the herring well and set aside. Discard any onions or other ingredients packed with the herring.

♦ Put the raspberry vinegar, onions, pepper, tarragon and white wine in a large glass or ceramic, but not metal, bowl. Add the herring, which should be completely covered by the liquid; if not, add equal amounts of white wine and vinegar until the herring is covered. Cover and chill for at least 12 hours.

♦ Just before serving, add the peas to the herring and marinade and mix gently.

Zakuski: Stuffed Peppers

SERVES 4—8

4 large green peppers

450 g/1 lb minced beef

25 g/1 oz cooked rice

1 small onion, finely chopped

¼ tsp salt

½ tsp black pepper

1 egg yolk

60 ml/2 fl oz red wine

50 g/2 oz chopped mushrooms

80 g/3 oz seeded and chopped fresh tomatoes

60 ml/2 fl oz fresh lemon juice

2 tbsp sugar

¼ tsp paprika

2 tbsp brandy

1½ tsp raspberry or cider vinegar

Preheat the oven to 190°C/375°F/Gas 5. Cut the tops off the green peppers and carefully discard the seeds. Blanch the peppers in a large pot of boiling water for 3 minutes. Drain well and set aside.

♦ In a large mixing bowl combine the minced beef, rice, onion, salt, pepper, egg yolk, wine and half the mushrooms. Mix well. Stuff the blanched peppers with the mixture.

♦ Place the peppers on their sides in a large baking dish. Add the vinegar and enough water to fill the dish to a depth of 5 cm/2 in. Cover and bake for 35 minutes.

♦ When the peppers have been in the oven for 30 minutes, combine the remaining mushrooms with the tomatoes, lemon juice, sugar, paprika and brandy in a small saucepan. Cover the saucepan and simmer over a very low heat for 5 minutes. Pour the mixture over the stuffed peppers.

♦ Reduce the oven temperature to 150°C/300°F/Gas 2. Bake the stuffed peppers, uncovered, for a further 15 minutes. Serve warm.

Russian Egg Drop Soup

SERVES 8—10

1.75 L/3¼ pt chicken stock

meat from ½ chicken, cooked and shredded

60 ml/2 fl oz white wine

225 g/8 oz fine egg noodles

½ tsp salt

¼ tsp dill

80 g/3 oz finely chopped celery

2 large carrots, quartered

1 sprig parsley

4 eggs, well beaten

Pour the chicken stock into a large saucepan. Add the chicken meat, wine, egg noodles, dill, salt, celery, carrots and parsley. Bring the soup to the boil. Reduce the heat and simmer for 18 to 20 minutes over a low heat.
♦ Bring the soup back to a furious boil. Beat the eggs in with a fork. Remove the pan from the heat when the eggs become cloud-like. Serve hot.

Cholent

SERVES 8—10

Of all the recipes ever collected for this legendary Jewish dish, no two are exactly alike. All involve some variation on beans, beef and potatoes, with some versions including barley as well. Cholent was traditionally prepared on Friday afternoon and then taken to the baker's oven, where it was cooked slowly in the banked fires until Saturday afternoon, when it was removed and served as the Sabbath meal.

225 g/½ lb flageolet beans

225 g/½ lb red kidney beans

225 g/½ lb yellow split peas

225 g/½ lb lentils

50 g/2 oz margarine

4 large onions, quartered

2 garlic cloves, crushed

1 tsp black pepper

1 tsp salt

2 tsp paprika

1.8 kg/4 lb beef brisket

750 ml/1¼ pt white wine

675 g/1½ lb potatoes, peeled and quartered

Preheat the oven to 230°C/450°F/Gas 8. Place the flageolet beans, red kidney beans, yellow split peas and lentils in separate bowls. Add 750 ml/1¼ pt of cold water to each bowl and leave the pulses to soak overnight. Drain well.
♦ Melt the margarine in a large flameproof casserole. Add the onions and brown them. Add the garlic, pepper, salt and paprika. Add the brisket and brown it.
♦ Add the wine, 950 ml/32 fl oz cold water, all the pulses and the potatoes. Bring the liquid to a boil. Cover the pot tightly and place it in the oven. Bake for 1 hour, then reduce the heat to 150°C/300°F/Gas 2 and bake for a further 90 minutes.
♦ Remove the brisket from the pot and let it rest for 10 minutes before slicing. Arrange the pulses and potatoes around the brisket and spoon over the broth.

Cabbage Salad

SERVES 8

This light, crisp dish is a welcome contrast to the hearty flavours of the cholent. Be sure the cabbage is fresh and the salad is served well chilled.

675 g/1½ lb white cabbage, shredded
1 small onion, diced
4 tbsp chopped spring onions
2 tbsp diced chilli peppers
½ tsp salt
4 tbsp chopped fresh coriander
3 tbsp olive oil
125 ml/4 fl oz lime juice
1 tbsp Dijon-style mustard
1 tbsp honey

Combine all the ingredients in a large serving bowl and toss well. Chill for 20 to 30 minutes before serving.

Russian Seedcake

MAKES 1 CAKE

This simple yet deliciously aromatic cake is the perfect ending to any meal. Serve it with Russian-style tea — stir a spoonful of preserves or rum, or both, into each glass of tea.

450 g/1 lb sugar
450 g/1 lb unsalted butter
10 eggs
450 g/1 lb flour
1 tsp salt
2 tsp baking powder
3 tsp vanilla essence
2 tbsp sesame seeds
2 tbsp caraway seeds
125 ml/4 fl oz orange juice
½ tsp cinnamon
125 g/4 oz raspberry or plum preserves

Preheat the oven to 180°C/350°F/Gas 4. Cream the sugar and butter together in a large mixing bowl. Add the eggs, two at a time, beating well after each addition.
♦ Add the flour, salt, baking powder, vanilla essence, sesame seeds, caraway seeds, orange juice and cinnamon. Beat for 7 minutes. Butter and flour a 30 cm/12 in diameter cake tin. Pour in the batter and bake for 1 hour or until a cocktail stick inserted in the centre of the cake comes out clean.
♦ Remove the cake from the oven and leave it to cool to room temperature. Spread the top of the cake with raspberry or plum preserves and serve.

Russian Dairy Lunch

This dairy lunch of traditional Russian specialities might have been served in the cosmopolitan home of a wealthy family or as a festive meal in a poorer household. The Russians are particularly fond of mushrooms in any form. This menu uses both dried and pickled mushrooms. The dessert, assuming anyone has room for it, is the famed Charlotte Russe.

Gefilte Fish Russe

Kasha

Fish Soup

Bliny

Soured Cream

Charlotte Russe

Gefilte Fish Russe

SERVES 8—10

Gefilte fish is a staple of Jewish cooking throughout Europe, Russia and America. It is made a little differently by each group, and each group claims to have originated the dish and to have the best recipe. The dish was originally made as the stuffing for baked fish. Eventually the stuffing itself became the dish.

900 g/2 lb fresh white fish fillets (set aside the heads, skin and bones)

900 g/2 lb fresh carp fillets (set aside the heads, skin and bones)

900 g/2 lb fresh pike fillets (set aside the heads, skin and bones)

2 tbsp salt

4 large onions, finely chopped

4 eggs, beaten

8 tbsp matzoh meal

2 tbsp sugar

2 carrots, cut into fine julienne strips

3 carrots, peeled and cut into 2.5 cm/1 in slices

Put the reserved fish heads, skin and bones into a large stock pot. Add 1.75 L/$3\frac{1}{4}$ pt cold water, 1 teaspoon salt and $1\frac{1}{2}$ teaspoons black pepper. Bring the liquid to a boil and cook, uncovered, over a high heat for 40 minutes. Pour the fish stock through a sieve into another pot and discard the heads, skin and bones.

♦ Finely chop the fish fillets. Put the chopped fish into a large bowl and add the onions, eggs, matzoh meal, sugar, remaining salt and pepper, julienne strips of carrot and 225 ml/8 fl oz cold water. Mix well until the consistency is even. Shape the fish mixture into balls about 5 cm/2 in in diameter.

♦ Bring the sieved fish stock to a boil over a low heat. Add the carrot slices. Drop the fish balls into the stock and cover the pot. Simmer over a low heat for 1 hour. Remove the cover and simmer for another 45 minutes. Remove the pot from the heat and let the gefilte fish cool in the liquid to room temperature.

♦ Remove the gefilte fish and put them into a glass or ceramic serving bowl. Pour the stock through a sieve again and pour it over the fish. Add the sliced carrots from the stock. Cover the bowl and chill for 2 hours before serving. Serve with horseradish.

Kasha

SERVES 8—10

Few foods are as deceiving as kasha. In Russia, kasha can mean any cereal; outside Russia, it almost always means buckwheat groats. Kasha sounds plain, mealy and unappetizing, but is in fact savoury and flavourful. Packaged, roasted buckwheat groats are available in many shops, in three types: fine, medium and coarse. For true authenticity, use coarse groats. This dish can be made with fresh mushrooms only, but the rich aroma from the dried mushrooms should not be missed.

225 g/8 oz dried mushrooms

225 g/8 oz kasha (coarse buckwheat groats)

2 eggs, beaten

$1\frac{1}{2}$ tsp salt

1 L/2 pt boiling water

225 g/$\frac{1}{2}$ lb butter

350 g/12 oz small onions, quartered

225 g/8 oz fresh mushrooms, quartered

2 tbsp finely chopped spring onions

Put the dried mushrooms into a small bowl and add enough warm water to cover. Let the mushrooms soak for 1 hour. Drain well. Trim away any tough stems and cut any large mushrooms in half.

♦ Put the kasha into a medium-sized mixing bowl. Fold the beaten eggs into the kasha.

♦ In a large, heavy frying pan, fry the kasha and egg mixture over a medium heat, until the kasha begins to become dry. Add the salt, 950 ml/32 fl oz of the boiling water and 125 g/4 oz of the butter. Cover the pan tightly and reduce the heat to low. Simmer for 20 minutes, stirring at 5-minute intervals.

♦ Add the remaining boiling water to the pan. Cover and simmer for a further 5 minutes. Turn the heat off. Leave it to stand for 15 minutes.

♦ Turn the heat on again and add the onions, dried mushrooms, fresh mushrooms and spring onions. Stir briefly. Reduce the heat to medium and add the remaining butter. Cook, stirring constantly, until the mushrooms are cooked and the kasha is dry again, about 3 to 5 minutes.

Fish Soup

SERVES 8—10

Deliciously light and savoury, this Russian fish soup is traditionally made during the summer and autumn months.

1.65 L/2¾ pt water

225 g/8 oz finely chopped onions

2 tsp finely chopped fresh parsley

¼ tsp finely grated lemon rind

1 bay leaf

¼ tsp black pepper

450 g/1 lb halibut steaks, cut into pieces

450 g/1 lb swordfish steaks, cut into pieces

150 ml/¼ pt double cream

225 ml/8 fl oz white wine

¼ tsp white pepper

1 garlic clove, crushed

2 large cucumbers, peeled and cut into slices

350 g/12 oz tomatoes, peeled, seeded and cut into pieces

80 g/3 oz black olives, stoned and halved

In a very large soup pot, combine the water, onions, parsley, lemon rind, bay leaf and black pepper. Bring the liquid to a boil, reduce the heat and simmer for 2 minutes.

♦ Add the fish to the pot and simmer for 5 minutes. Reduce the heat to low and simmer for a further 5 minutes.

♦ Add the cream, white wine, white pepper, garlic clove, cucumbers and tomatoes to the pot. Simmer over a low heat for 5 minutes. Do not let the soup boil.

♦ Remove the pot from the heat. Stir in the olives. Leave the soup to stand for 30 seconds. Stir again and serve.

Bliny

SERVES 6

Bliny are a distinctly Russian dish. They are a bit like pancakes or crêpes, and even bear a close family resemblance to blintzes (see page 208), but all comparisons end there. Any smoked fish can be substituted for the mackerel. The batter takes some time to prepare. Once it is ready, it should be used immediately. Use plenty of butter.

225 ml/8 fl oz lukewarm water
50 g/2 oz active dry yeast
350 g/12 oz buckwheat flour
450 g/1 lb plain white flour
950 ml/32 fl oz warm milk
6 egg yolks, beaten
3 tsp sugar
900 ml/1½ pt soured cream (see below)
1 tsp salt
450 g/1 lb butter, clarified and cooled
6 egg whites
900 g/2 lb smoked mackerel

Put the lukewarm water in a shallow bowl. Sprinkle the yeast over the water. Leave it to stand for 3 minutes and then stir until the yeast is completely dissolved. Put the bowl in a warm dry place for 5 minutes.

♦ Combine the buckwheat and white flour in a large mixing bowl. Make a well in the centre of the flour and pour in the yeast. Add half of the warm milk.

♦ Stir well and then beat vigorously until the mixture is even and smooth. Cover the bowl with a clean cloth and set aside in a warm dry place for 3 hours.

♦ Remove the cloth and stir the bliny mixture vigorously. Cover the bowl again and return it to the warm dry place. Leave it to stand for 1¾ hours.

♦ Stir in the remaining milk and the egg yolks, sugar, 6 tablespoons of the soured cream, salt and 80 g/3 oz of the clarified butter. Beat until the mixture is smooth.

♦ In another bowl, beat the egg whites until they are stiff. Gradually fold the egg whites into the bliny batter. Leave it to stand for 40 minutes.

♦ Preheat the oven to 130°C/250°F/Gas ½. Coat the bottom of a very large, heavy frying pan with 50 g/2 oz of the clarified butter and place over a high heat.

♦ Add 3 tablespoons of the bliny batter. Tilt the pan to coat it with a thin layer of the batter. Cook the bliny for 2 to 3 minutes on each side. When the pancake is done, transfer it to a ceramic or glass dish with a tight lid and keep warm in oven. Repeat with the remaining batter, adding more butter as needed.

♦ To serve the bliny, first brush each one with clarified butter, place a wedge of smoked mackerel on the bliny, fold it over and top with a spoonful of soured cream.

Soured Cream

MAKES 1.5 L/2½ PT

Russian-style soured cream is somewhat thinner than that sold commercially. This easy recipe for homemade soured cream is close to the authentic style, and is far more flavourful than the commercial equivalent.

350 ml/12 fl oz buttermilk
1.4 l/48 fl oz double cream

Combine the buttermilk and cream in a large jar with a tightly fitting lid. Close tightly and shake vigorously for 90 seconds. Leave it to stand at room temperature for 2 days. Refrigerate for 2½ days before using.

Charlotte Russe

SERVES 8

The great French chef Antoine Carême created this celebrated dessert after visiting Russia in the mid-nineteenth century.

16 sponge fingers, halved lengthwise

4 egg yolks

125 g/4 oz sugar

225 ml/8 fl oz milk

1 scant tbsp vanilla essence

1½ tbsp unflavoured gelatine, dissolved in 60 ml/2 fl oz cold water

125 ml/4 fl oz soured cream

125 ml/4 fl oz double cream, chilled

1 tbsp Triple Sec liqueur

600 g/1¼ lb frozen raspberries, thawed and drained

3 tbsp castor sugar

2 tbsp blackberry brandy

Set 16 sponge finger halves aside. Take the remaining sponge fingers and cut diagonal slices from each side of one end, so that one end of each is still curved and the other comes to a point.

♦ In a 1-L/32-fl oz pudding mould, arrange the trimmed sponge finger halves at the bottom so that their points touch and their diagonal edges are side by side. The pattern on the bottom of the pudding mould should resemble a doily with bevelled edges. Place the remaining untrimmed sponge finger halves against the side of the mould, standing them straight up. Try not to leave any gaps between the untrimmed sponge finger halves.

♦ In a mixing bowl, beat the egg yolks. Gradually beat in the sugar. Continue beating until the sugar is fully incorporated into the egg yolks.

♦ Warm the milk and vanilla essence in a small saucepan over a low heat. When the milk starts to bubble, beat it into the egg mixture.

♦ Pour the egg and milk mixture back into the saucepan. Cook over a low heat, stirring all the time, until the mixture becomes a thick custard. Do not let the mixture boil. Stir in the dissolved gelatine. When the mixture has an even consistency throughout, pour it through a fine sieve into a mixing bowl.

♦ In another bowl, whip the soured cream and double cream together until the mixture begins to stiffen.

♦ Place the bowl containing the custard mixture inside a larger bowl. Put ice cubes and cold water into the larger bowl until it comes halfway up the sides of the custard bowl. Stir the custard with a metal spoon until it begins to thicken noticeably.

♦ Fold the whipped cream mixture into the custard, breaking up any lumps with a whisk or fork. Stir in the Triple Sec liqueur.

♦ Pour the contents of the custard bowl into the mould lined with sponge fingers. Chill for 5 to 6 hours before serving.

♦ Blend the sieved raspberries, castor sugar and blackberry brandy together in a small bowl. Spoon the sauce over slices of the Charlotte Russe just before serving.

Russian Chanuka Dinner

The main course at a traditional Russian Chanuka Dinner is almost always pickled beef tongue or other pickled meat. It is also customary to end the meal with a sweet fruit dessert. Potato pancakes, however, the one dish that most Jews now associate with Chanuka, would not be served (but see page 217 for a recipe).

Hearty Beef Soup
Pickled Beef Tongue
Glazed Chicken Wings
Braised Carrots and Onions
Cucumber Salad
Fruit Kisel

Hearty Beef Soup

SERVES 8

This hearty beef soup provides considerable protection from the inside out against the rigours of a severe Russian winter.

450 g/1 lb beef brisket or flank, thinly sliced
225 g/½ lb beef bones, split into pieces
1 large turnip, cut into pieces
1 onion, quartered
2 celery stalks, finely chopped
1 carrot, halved
3 tbsp chopped green pepper
¼ tsp salt
¼ tsp black pepper
4 tbsp chopped fresh chives
60 ml/2 fl oz red wine
450 ml/¾ pt water
225 g/8 oz egg noodles

Put all the ingredients except the noodles into a large soup pot. Bring to a boil, reduce the heat and simmer, tightly covered, for 5 to 6 hours. Add the noodles. Raise the heat to medium and cook for a further 12 to 15 minutes. Serve hot.

Pickled Beef Tongue

SERVES 8

To a Russian Jew of the late nineteenth century, this dish meant Chanuka.

1.8-2.3 kg/4-5 lb smoked beef tongue
450 ml/¾ pt white wine vinegar
3 large onions, quartered
175 g/6 oz sugar
1 bay leaf
1 whole clove
¼ tsp white pepper
2 tbsp honey
¼ tsp cinnamon
2 tbsp pickling spice, tied up in muslin

In a large pot, cover the smoked beef tongue with water. Bring the water to a boil. Skim off the fat that rises to the surface. Reduce the heat to low and cover the pan. Simmer for 3 to 4 hours, or until tender, depending on the size of the tongue. Remove the pot from the heat and leave the tongue to cool in the liquid. Skim off the fat.
♦ Put 750 ml/1¼ pt of the cooking liquid into a saucepan. Discard the remaining cooking liquid or save it for stock. Add the vinegar, onions, sugar, bay leaf, clove, white pepper, honey and cinnamon. Bring the mixture to a boil and simmer for 5 minutes. Add the pickling spice. Remove the clove and simmer for a further 5 minutes. Remove the bay leaf and spice bag. Pour the liquid over the tongue. Chill for at least 1½ hours and serve.

Glazed Chicken Wings

SERVES 8

Sweet foods are traditional on Chanuka.

> 1.4 kg/3 lb chicken wings
>
> 4 tbsp tomato sauce
>
> $\frac{1}{2}$ tsp garlic powder
>
> $\frac{1}{2}$ tsp onion powder
>
> $\frac{1}{4}$ tsp ground ginger
>
> $\frac{1}{4}$ tsp cayenne pepper
>
> 125 ml/4 fl oz white wine
>
> 4 tbsp honey
>
> 4 tbsp apricot preserves
>
> 2 tbsp peach preserves

Preheat the oven to 190°C/375°F/Gas 5. Cut the tips from the wings (discard or save them for stock). Spread the chicken wings in one layer in a large greased pan. Bake for 30 minutes.

♦ Meanwhile, mix together the tomato sauce, garlic powder, onion powder, ginger, cayenne pepper and wine in a small bowl.

♦ Spoon the mixture over the chicken wings and bake for a further 30 minutes. While the wings are cooking, mix together the honey, apricot and peach preserves in a small bowl. Brush the glaze over the chicken wings. Raise the heat to 200°C/400°F/Gas 6. Bake for a further 10 to 15 minutes, or until the wings are golden and glazed.

Braised Carrots and Onions

SERVES 6—8

The natural sweetness of carrots and their golden colour was thought to represent good luck on festive occasions.

> 4 tbsp margarine
>
> 1 medium onion, sliced into rings
>
> 4 tbsp finely chopped spring onions
>
> 2 large tomatoes, cut into eighths and seeded
>
> 16 baby carrots, scraped and cut into quarters
>
> $\frac{1}{4}$ tsp salt
>
> $\frac{1}{4}$ tsp ground white pepper
>
> 1 tbsp chopped fresh coriander
>
> 2 tbsp chopped fresh parsley

Melt the margarine in a large saucepan over a low heat. Add the onion and spring onions. Fry, stirring constantly, for 5 minutes. Add the tomatoes and raise the heat to medium. Fry, stirring constantly for a further 3 to 4 minutes.

♦ Add the carrots, salt and white pepper, coriander and parsley. Reduce the heat to low. Cook for 1 to 2 minutes stirring constantly. Cover the saucepan and reduce the heat to very low. Simmer for 5 minutes and serve.

Cucumber Salad

SERVES 8

Cucumbers or pickles feature in many Russian dishes. This salad, which is slightly wilted when served, still has a delicious crunch to it.

3 large cucumbers, peeled and thinly sliced

450 ml/$\frac{3}{4}$ pt red wine vinegar

$\frac{1}{2}$ tsp celery salt

$\frac{1}{2}$ head lettuce, shredded

1 tbsp honey

$\frac{1}{4}$ tsp black pepper

$\frac{1}{2}$ tsp fresh dill, chopped

4 tbsp olive oil

1 tsp Dijon-style mustard

Toss all the ingredients thoroughly in a large salad bowl: Chill for 2 hours before serving.

Fruit Kisel

SERVES 8—10

Kisel is a cold, thick liquid dessert very popular in Russia. There are many different recipes, and there are no hard and fast rules about ingredients. Try different combinations of fruit, making sure to mash the fruit into a smooth purée. More potato starch may be needed to thicken the kisel if very juicy fresh fruits are used.

225 g/$\frac{1}{2}$ lb tart red apples, peeled, cored and cut into small chunks

125 g/$\frac{1}{4}$ lb dried apricots

700 g/1$\frac{1}{2}$ lb fresh or thawed frozen strawberries

1 L/1$\frac{3}{4}$ pt cold water

125 ml/4 fl oz jellied cranberry sauce

225 g/8 oz sugar

1$\frac{1}{2}$ tbsp potato starch, dissolved in 2 tbsp cold water

Place the apples, apricots and strawberries in a large saucepan. Add the cranberry sauce and cold water and bring the mixture to a boil over a high heat. Reduce the heat to low and simmer uncovered for 15 minutes, stirring occasionally.

♦ With the back of a spoon, press the fruit mixture through a fine sieve into a large mixing bowl. Discard any solids that remain in the sieve. Stir in the sugar.

♦ Put the fruit and sugar mixture into a large saucepan and bring it to a boil. Reduce the heat to medium and stir in the potato starch mixture. Cook until the purée returns to a boil. Remove the saucepan from the heat and let the purée cool to room temperature.

♦ Spoon the purée into pudding or tulip glasses. Chill for 4 hours before serving.

Russian Dinner

This average weekday meal consists of only five courses, a very small number in the heyday of Russian Jewish cuisine.

Sorrel and Kidney Soup
Fried Spinach
Stuffed Veal Shoulder
Merchant's Spiced Potatoes
Strawberry Peach Sorbet

Sorrel and Kidney Soup

SERVES 6—8

Kidneys, which have lost some of their attraction in modern times, were considered a delicacy by most Slavs and Europeans. They are shown at their best in this traditional Russian soup.

4 tbsp margarine

150 g/5 oz small onions, quartered

150 g/5 oz chopped celery

1 large pickled cucumber, finely chopped

6 tbsp finely chopped parsley

700 g/1½ lb fresh sorrel leaves, stemmed and chopped

225 g/½ lb fresh spinach, coarsely chopped

1 tsp salt

1 tsp black pepper

1.75 L/3¼ pt chicken stock

450 g/1 lb veal kidneys

25 g/1 oz flour

2 tbsp olive oil

2 egg yolks, beaten

In a large casserole, melt 3 tablespoons of the margarine. Reduce the heat to low and stir in the onions and celery. Cover and simmer for 8 minutes.

♦ Add the pickled cucumber, parsley, sorrel, spinach, salt and pepper. Stir and cook over a low heat for 2 minutes. Add the chicken stock and raise the heat to high. Bring the mixture to a boil. Reduce the heat and simmer for 25 minutes.

♦ While the stock simmers, trim the fat off the kidneys and cut them crosswise into 1 cm/½ in thick slices. Dredge the slices lightly in the flour.

♦ Heat the remaining tablespoon of margarine and the olive oil in a large, heavy frying pan over a medium heat. When the mixture begins to brown, add the kidney slices. Fry, stirring constantly, for 4 to 6 minutes, or until the slices are browned. Add the kidney slices to the stock and simmer for 10 minutes.

♦ Add the egg yolks to the soup, stirring constantly. Simmer for a further 3 minutes and serve.

Fried Spinach

SERVES 6—8

This novel way to prepare fresh spinach originated in Riga. It is popular with Jews throughout Russia and the Ukraine. It should only be made with fresh spinach.

3 tbsp groundnut oil

2 garlic cloves, diced

1 small onion, finely chopped

900 g/2 lb fresh spinach, thoroughly washed and shredded

60 ml/2 fl oz white wine

¼ tsp salt

Heat the oil in a large, heavy frying pan. Add the garlic and onion and fry, stirring constantly, over a moderate heat for 2 minutes.

♦ Reduce the heat to low. Add the spinach, wine and salt. Cook, stirring constantly, until the spinach is wilted and bright green, about 3 minutes.

Stuffed Veal Shoulder

SERVES 6—8

This succulent main course combines the flavour of three different meats. It's a good dish for any religious or secular holiday meal.

450 g/1 lb minced veal

125 g/¼ lb lean minced beef

225 g/½ lb minced chicken

80 g/3 oz finely chopped onion

4 tbsp finely chopped spring onions

20 g/¾ oz soft breadcrumbs

450 ml/¾ pt cold water

2 eggs

1 tsp salt

½ tsp white pepper

1.8-2.3 kg/4-5 lb veal shoulder, boned

1 garlic clove, crushed

4 hard-boiled eggs

6 tbsp margarine

In a large mixing bowl, combine the minced veal, minced beef, minced chicken, onion, spring onions, breadcrumbs, water, eggs, salt and pepper. Mix thoroughly until the stuffing has an even consistency.

♦ Preheat the oven to 190°C/375°F/Gas 5.

♦ With a sharp knife, cut the veal shoulder almost in half horizontally, where it is thickest. The veal shoulder should lie flat on a large cutting board. Rub the cut surface of the veal with the garlic clove and then cover it with a large piece of greaseproof paper. Beat the veal with a meat pounder until the meat is flattened.

♦ Remove the paper and spread half the flattened veal shoulder with half the stuffing mixture. Arrange the hard-boiled eggs on top of the stuffing. Spread the remaining stuffing mixture over the eggs.

♦ Fold the veal over and tie with strong kitchen string at 5 cm/2 in intervals.

♦ Place the veal in a shallow roasting tin filled with 5 cm/2 in water. Roast for 2 hours. Remove the veal from the oven. Remove the roast from the tin and put it on a carving board. Cut and remove the string. Let the roast stand for 10 minutes before slicing.

♦ Melt the margarine in a small saucepan. Add the drippings from the roasting tin. Stir well and simmer for 10 minutes, uncovered, until the gravy is slightly reduced and thickened. Serve the gravy separately.

RUSSIA AND EASTERN EUROPE

Merchant's Spiced Potatoes

SERVES 6—8

This traditional Russian dish shows a pronounced Eastern influence. It uses spices that at one time only a merchant could afford.

> 2 tbsp vegetable oil
> $\frac{1}{2}$ tsp mustard
> 1 tomato, seeded and finely chopped
> 4 tbsp green pepper, diced
> $\frac{1}{4}$ tsp cayenne pepper
> $\frac{1}{4}$ tsp ground turmeric
> $\frac{1}{4}$ tsp ground allspice
> $\frac{1}{4}$ tsp ground ginger
> $\frac{1}{4}$ tsp salt
> $\frac{1}{2}$ tsp sugar
> $\frac{1}{4}$ tsp ground coriander
> 5 large boiled potatoes, cut into chunks

Heat the oil in a large, heavy frying pan over a moderate heat. Add the mustard, tomato, green pepper, cayenne pepper, turmeric, allspice, ginger, salt, sugar and coriander. Cook, stirring constantly, for 2 minutes.
♦ Add the potatoes and cook, stirring constantly, until the potatoes are coated with the spices and heated through, about 5 minutes.

Strawberry Peach Sorbet

SERVES 6—8

Fruit sorbets, which were perfected by the Austrians, quickly became a favourite dessert among the Russian Jews. Since sorbets contain no milk, they can be served with either dairy or meat meals.

> 4 large peaches
> 450 g/1 lb fresh strawberries, chopped
> 60 ml/2 fl oz fresh lemon juice
> 175 g/6 oz castor sugar

Bring 750 ml/1$\frac{1}{4}$ pt water to a boil in a medium-sized pan. Add the peaches and cook for 2 minutes.
♦ Remove the peaches from the pot and drain well. When the peaches are cool enough to handle, remove the skins and stones. Mash the peaches into a pulp in a large mixing bowl.
♦ Purée the peach pulp, strawberries and lemon juice in a liquidizer or food processor.
♦ Stir the sugar into the fruit mixture and purée for another 10 to 15 seconds. Pour the mixture into a large, shallow dish and freeze until hard. Remove the dish from the freezer 1 hour before serving and let the sorbet soften in the refrigerator.

Russian Dairy Lunch

This four-course Russian dairy lunch features two Russian specialities:
a flaky salmon loaf and a borscht, Moscow-style.

Moscow Borscht
Vegetables in Vinaigrette
Salmon Loaf
Apple Charlotte

Moscow Borscht

SERVES 8

Where there are Russians, there is borscht — hot or cold, with or without sausages, with or without beef stock. The variations on the theme are almost endless. This deliciously light and flavourful dairy variation calls for swordfish meat and vegetable stock.

40 ml/$1\frac{1}{2}$ oz butter

70 g/$2\frac{1}{2}$ oz chopped onion

1.75 L/$3\frac{1}{4}$ pt vegetable stock

900g/2 lb beetroot, peeled and cut into 5 mm/$\frac{1}{4}$ in rounds

4 tbsp chopped spring onions

3 tbsp lemon juice

60 ml/2 fl oz red wine vinegar

1 large swordfish steak, cubed

1 tsp salt

$\frac{1}{2}$ tsp white pepper

60 ml/2 fl oz white wine

4 sprigs of parsley

1 bay leaf

225 g/$\frac{1}{2}$ lb white cabbage, shredded

2 tomatoes, peeled, seeded and chopped

25 g/1 oz finely chopped fresh dill

soured cream

In a large soup pot, melt the butter over a moderate heat. Add the chopped onions and fry until they are browned, about 4 to 5 minutes. Add the vegetable stock, beetroot, spring onions, lemon juice, vinegar, swordfish cubes, salt and white pepper. Simmer for 25 minutes.

♦ Add the white wine, parsley, bay leaf, cabbage, tomatoes and dill. Reduce the heat to low and simmer for a further 50 minutes.

♦ Swirl a tablespoon of soured cream into each bowl and serve.

Vegetables in Vinaigrette

SERVES 8

450 g/1 lb fresh asparagus

1 large head fresh broccoli, cut into florets

1 large tin artichoke hearts, drained

For the dressing:

125 ml/4 fl oz red wine vinegar

125 ml/4 fl oz olive oil

2 tbsp chopped spring onions

2 tbsp Dijon-style mustard

$\frac{1}{2}$ tsp dried chives

2 tbsp honey

$\frac{1}{2}$ tsp celery salt

$\frac{1}{4}$ tsp black pepper

$\frac{1}{4}$ tsp ground white pepper

1 garlic clove, finely chopped

Cook the asparagus in a large, covered pan of boiling water until they are tender, about 10 to 12 minutes. Cook the broccoli florets in a large pan of boiling water until they are tender but still crisp, about 7 minutes. Drain well.

♦ Put the asparagus, broccoli and artichoke hearts into a large bowl, cover and chill for 40 minutes.

♦ In another bowl, combine the vinegar, olive oil, spring onions, mustard, chives, honey, salt, black pepper, white pepper and garlic. Mix well. Chill for 40 minutes.

♦ Stir the dressing well and pour it over the vegetables.

Salmon Loaf

SERVES 8

600 g/1$\frac{1}{4}$ lb flour

225 g/8 oz unsalted butter, softened

80 g/4 oz white vegetable fat

2 tsp salt

225 ml/8 fl oz iced water

900 g/2 lb fresh salmon, skinned and boned

450 g/1 lb cabbage, shredded

225 g/8 oz roughly chopped onion

1 tsp black pepper

350 ml/12 fl oz white wine

450 g/1 lb mushrooms, quartered

2 egg yolks

225 ml/8 fl oz chicken stock

4 tbsp lemon juice

4 tbsp chopped fresh dill

4 hard-boiled eggs, chopped

2 tbsp sugar

In a large mixing bowl, combine the flour, 175 g/6 oz butter, white vegetable fat and 1 teaspoon salt. Mix together with a wooden spoon until the dough has a flaky texture. Add the iced water and mix until smooth. Divide the dough into 2 equal portions. Wrap each half in clingfilm and refrigerate for $3\frac{1}{2}$ hours.

♦ Put the salmon, remaining butter, cabbage, onion, pepper, wine, mushrooms, remaining salt, egg yolks, chicken stock, lemon juice, dill and sugar into a large saucepan. Simmer for 1 hour, or until most of the liquid has evaporated.

♦ Flake the salmon with a fork. Stir gently and add the chopped hard-boiled eggs. Stir gently again. Set the mixture aside.

♦ Roll out half the chilled dough on a lightly-floured surface into a rectangle about 2.5 cm/1 in thick. Dust with flour, and then roll the dough out into a sheet 3 mm/$\frac{1}{8}$ in thick. Trim the sheet into a rectangle 20 cm × 40 cm/8 in × 16 in. Repeat with the remaining dough, but trim the sheet to 25 cm × 40 cm/10 in × 16 in.

♦ Place the smaller dough rectangle on a large, greased baking sheet. Arrange the salmon filling evenly over the dough sheet, leaving a 2.5 cm/1 in border around the edges. Place the larger dough sheet over the filling. Press the edges of the top and bottom dough sheets together with a fork. Chill for 15 minutes.

♦ Preheat the oven to 200°C/400°F/Gas 6. Bake the loaf for 1 hour. Serve immediately.

Apple Charlotte

SERVES 8

There are many kinds of charlotte. Apple charlotte, one of the simpler versions, is popular as a lunchtime dish.

25 g/1 oz unsalted butter, softened
350 g/12 oz unsalted butter, clarified
12 large slices of white bread, halved, crusts removed
1.4 kg/3 lb tart apples, peeled, cored and chopped
1.4 kg/3 lb sweet apples, peeled, cored and chopped
350 g/12 oz sugar
125 ml/4 fl oz water
2 tbsp lime juice
2 tbsp lemon juice
1 tsp cinnamon
900 g/2 lb apricot preserves
60 ml/2 fl oz apricot brandy
60 ml/2 fl oz orange juice
$\frac{1}{4}$ tsp vanilla essence

Rub the softened butter over the inside surface of a pudding mould.

♦ Put the clarified butter into a large mixing bowl. Dip the bread into the butter and line the sides and bottom of the pudding mould with them.

♦ Combine the apples, sugar, water, lemon juice and lime juice in a large flameproof casserole. Bring the mixture to a boil, cover and simmer for 40 minutes over a low heat. Add the cinnamon and cook, uncovered, over a medium heat for a further 15 minutes. Chill the mixture for 1 hour.

♦ Gently pour the chilled apple mixture into the prepared pudding mould.

♦ Preheat the oven to 200°C/400°F/Gas 6. Bake the pudding for 1 hour. Cool for 30 minutes at room temperature.

♦ Invert the pudding on a large flat plate. Gently shake the mould to loosen the apple charlotte. Carefully pull the pudding mould away.

♦ In a small mixing bowl, combine the apricot preserves, apricot brandy, orange juice and vanilla essence. Spoon over the apple charlotte before serving.

Polish Yom Kippur

Yom Kippur, or the Day of Atonement, is a solemn fast day. A boiled dinner of several different specialities often used to be served before the holy day began.

Beef Chopped Liver
Chicken in the Pot with Soup
Kreplach
Matzoh Balls
Boiled Beef
Baked Apples

Beef Chopped Liver

SERVES 8

A variation on the more familiar chicken chopped liver, this recipe is a speciality of the Eastern European Jews.

125 ml/4 fl oz beef stock
450 g/1 lb fresh calf's liver, cubed
1 garlic clove, finely chopped
450 g/1 lb fresh chicken livers, halved
2 hard-boiled eggs, finely chopped
125 ml/4 fl oz mayonnaise
4 tbsp diced green pepper
1 large celery stalk, finely chopped
4 tbsp diced onion
2 tbsp sherry
1 tsp brandy
2 tbsp unflavoured dry breadcrumbs
$\frac{1}{2}$ tsp salt
1 tsp white pepper

Heat the beef stock in a medium-sized saucepan. Add the liver cubes and garlic and cook, stirring frequently, for 10 to 12 minutes, or until the liver is thoroughly cooked. Remove the liver cubes and set them aside. Discard the cooking liquid.
♦ Put the chicken livers in a saucepan and add enough cold water to cover. Bring the liquid to a boil and cook for 15 minutes. Drain well.
♦ Put the calf's liver cubes, chicken livers, eggs mayonnaise, green pepper, celery, onions, sherry, brandy, breadcrumbs, salt and white pepper into a large mixing bowl. Mash the ingredients together with a fork until the mixture has a fine and even consistency. Cover the bowl and refrigerate for at least 2 hours before serving.

Chicken in the Pot with Soup

SERVES 6—8

This dish, the queen of all chicken soups, is served with kreplach and matzoh balls. The kreplach, matzoh balls and fine egg noodles should be prepared separately and combined just before serving.

2 large parsley sprigs
1 large parsnip
1 small leek
1 dill sprig
3 L/5$\frac{1}{2}$ pt water
2 celery stalks, halved
2 large onions, halved
5 carrots, halved
1.4 kg/3 lb chicken, cut into pieces
1 tsp salt
$\frac{1}{2}$ tsp black pepper
$\frac{1}{4}$ tsp ground white pepper
50 g/2 oz fine egg noodles

Tie the parsley, parsnip, leek and dill together with kitchen string.

♦ Fill a large soup pot with the water. Add the bunch of vegetables and herbs and the celery, onions, carrots and chicken pieces. Bring the liquid to a boil. Add the salt, black pepper and white pepper. Reduce the heat to low. Simmer for 1 hour 45 minutes.

♦ Remove and discard the bunch of vegetables and herbs. Add the egg noodles to the pot. Simmer for 10 minutes, stirring occasionally.

♦ Serve the soup with the vegetables and chicken pieces in large deep bowls.

Kreplach

MAKES ABOUT 50 KREPLACH

Kreplach in chicken soup are traditionally served on Purim and during Succoth, as well as at Yom Kippur Dinner.

900 g/2 lb boneless chuck steak, coarsely minced
4 small onions, coarsely chopped
60 ml/2 fl oz vegetable oil
$\frac{1}{2}$ tsp salt
$\frac{1}{2}$ tsp black pepper
450 g/1 lb fine wholemeal flour
2 eggs
350 ml/12 fl oz warm water

In a large saucepan, brown the meat and onions in the oil over a low heat for 8 to 10 minutes. Add $\frac{1}{4}$ teaspoon salt and the black pepper. Stir well. Remove from the heat and set aside.

♦ In a large mixing bowl, make the flour into a mound. Make a well in the flour. Sprinkle the remaining salt over the flour and break the eggs into the well. Beat with a whisk, gradually adding the warm water, until the consistency of the dough is smooth and even. Roll the dough into a ball.

♦ Cut the dough into approximately 15 equal pieces. One by one, roll each piece out into a thin sheet. Cut 3 rounds 7.5 cm/3 in in diameter from each sheet with a pastry cutter. Repeat the process until all the dough is used up.

♦ Place 1 teaspoon of the meat and onion filling in the centre of each dough round. Fold the dough over and seal the edges together with the blunt end of a spoon.

♦ Bring a very large pot of water to the boil. Drop in the kreplach, about 8 to 15 at a time, depending on the size of the pot. When the water returns to the boil, cook the kreplach for 3 to 5 minutes, or until they float to the top. Remove with a slotted spoon and set aside. If the kreplach are not being served within 30 minutes, refrigerate them. Add them to the chicken soup for 4 minutes before serving.

Matzoh Balls

SERVES 8

Also called knaidlach, matzoh balls are not just served for Passover.

4 eggs, separated
225 g/8 oz matzoh meal
$\frac{1}{2}$ tsp ground ginger
$\frac{1}{2}$ tsp ground white pepper
$\frac{1}{2}$ tsp salt
5 tbsp chicken fat
225 ml/8 fl oz hot chicken stock
3 L/5$\frac{1}{2}$ pt water

Beat the egg whites in a medium-sized mixing bowl until stiff. Set aside.
♦ In a large mixing bowl, combine the matzoh meal, ginger, pepper, and salt. Add the fat, stock and egg yolks. Fold in the egg whites and chill for 90 minutes.
♦ In a large soup pot, bring the water to a boil. Form the matzoh meal dough into balls with a diameter of about 4 cm/1½ in and drop them into the pot. Cover tightly and cook for 25 to 30 minutes. Do not remove the cover during this time. If the matzoh balls are not being used within 30 minutes, refrigerate them and add them to the chicken in the pot soup 5 minutes before serving.

Boiled Beef

SERVES 8

This substantial dish is remarkably simple to prepare. The method is ideal for making less expensive beef cuts tender and flavourful.

1.4 kg/3 lb beef flank

450 ml/¾ pt beef stock

450 ml/¾ pt chicken stock

450 ml/¾ pt white wine

3 large onions, quartered

1 parsley sprig

2 bay leaves

6 potatoes, peeled and quartered

4 large carrots, peeled and halved

450 g/1 lb green beans, trimmed and halved

5 small beets, peeled and quartered

1 large turnip, peeled and cubed

1 garlic clove, crushed

½ tsp salt

½ tsp black pepper

Put all the ingredients into a large, heavy pan. Simmer, covered, over a medium heat for 1 hour. Reduce the heat to low and simmer for 1 hour longer.
♦ Remove the beef from the pan and leave it to stand for 10 minutes before slicing. Serve the beef slices in bowls with the vegetables and stock ladled over them.

Baked Apples

SERVES 8

Although they are always called baked, the apples in this light dessert are steamed.

8 large red baking apples

4 whole cloves

1 tsp cinnamon

2 tsp sugar

2 tsp brown sugar

8 tbsp honey

Place 4 apples into each of two large pans with 150 ml/¾ pt cold water. Add 2 cloves, ½ teaspoon cinnamon, 1 teaspoon sugar, 1 teaspoon brown sugar and 4 tablespoons honey to each saucepan.
♦ Cover, and steam the apples for 5 minutes over a medium heat. Remove the cloves and steam for a further 5 minutes. Let the apples cool in their liquid for 10 to 15 minutes. Serve warm, with some of the cooking liquid spooned over each apple. The apples can also be chilled and served cold.

Polish Succoth Dinner

Succoth celebrates the harvest. In ancient Palestine, the harvesters would build booths (succoth) in the fields and spend the night in them. Today, many observant Jews still build a succah every year and at least eat dinner in it. Among the Polish Jews, the meal would be one with pungent, earthy flavours, what the Poles idiomatically call tam (pronounced 'tohm'). Braised country foods are traditional. So is the famous version of stuffed cabbage, perhaps because cabbage is abundant at harvest time.

Little Meatballs
Garlic Chicken Soup
Baal Shem Tov's Soup
Polish Stuffed Cabbage
Holiday Carrots
Berry Kuchen

Little Meatballs

SERVES 8

This classic Polish dish is often served on holidays. Unlike most of the recipes in this book, where there is a wide latitude for variation, this recipe should be followed exactly. Good quality beef chuck steak is recommended for best results.

900 g/2 lb beef chuck steak, minced

450 ml/$\frac{3}{4}$ pt chicken stock

2$\frac{1}{2}$ tbsp tomato purée

2$\frac{1}{2}$ tbsp grape jelly

$\frac{1}{2}$ tsp salt

$\frac{1}{4}$ tsp ground white pepper

1 garlic clove, finely chopped

$\frac{1}{2}$ tsp dried oregano

$\frac{1}{4}$ tsp dried rosemary

2 tbsp chicken fat

$\frac{1}{2}$ tsp dried dill

$\frac{1}{2}$ tsp dried basil

In a large mixing bowl combine the minced beef, tomato purée, 150 ml/$\frac{1}{4}$ pt of the chicken stock, grape jelly, salt, white pepper, garlic, oregano and rosemary. Mix well. Shape the mixture into meatballs approximately 2.5 cm/1 in in diameter.
♦ In a large saucepan, melt the chicken fat over a low heat. Add the meatballs and brown for 5 minutes. Add the remaining chicken stock and the dill and basil. Simmer for 15 minutes over a very low heat. Serve warm.

Garlic Chicken Soup

SERVES 8

The simple yet pungent flavour of this traditional country soup was thought to arouse the taste buds for the courses to follow. This recipe can be traced back at least as far as the seventeenth century.

1$\frac{1}{2}$ L/2$\frac{1}{2}$ pt chicken stock

60 ml/2 fl oz white wine

450 g/1 lb boned, skinned and shredded chicken

175 g/6 oz peeled and quartered garlic cloves

70 g/2$\frac{1}{2}$ oz chopped onion

1 tbsp chopped spring onions

Combine the chicken stock, white wine and shredded chicken meat in a medium-sized saucepan. Simmer over a low heat for 15 minutes.
♦ Add the garlic cloves, chopped onions and spring onions to the soup. Simmer for 10 to 12 minutes longer and serve. This soup is especially good with chunks of crusty French bread.

Baal Shem Tov's Soup

SERVES 8

*The Baal Shem Tov (Master of the Good Name) was Israel ben Eliezer (1700—60),
the founder of Hassidism. Much legend surrounds his life, but we know that he was
an orphan and that he was not very well educated. This bean soup is said to have
been a favourite of his.*

3 tbsp chicken fat
2 onions, chopped
150 g/5 oz chopped celery
2 parsley sprigs
1 bay leaf
$\frac{1}{2}$ tsp dried thyme
1 beef soup bone
1 kg/2$\frac{1}{4}$ lb cooked black-eyed beans
1.5 L/2$\frac{1}{2}$ pt beef stock
900 ml/32 fl oz water
salt to taste
black pepper to taste
4 tbsp brandy
2 tbsp lemon juice

Melt the chicken fat in a large pot. Add the onions, celery, parsley, bay leaf and
thyme. Cook over a low heat, stirring occasionally, for 10 minutes. Add the beef
bone, beans, beef stock, water, salt and pepper. Bring the liquid to a boil, reduce the
heat, and simmer for 3 hours. Add more water if needed.
♦ Remove and discard the beef bone, parsley sprigs and bay leaf. Add the brandy
and lemon juice and stir well. Add more water if necessary.

Polish Stuffed Cabbage

SERVES 8

This distinctly Polish variation on a traditional Jewish dish differs slightly from the Russian version. It is sure to delight all stuffed cabbage devotees.

1 large head white cabbage
450 g/1 lb minced beef sirloin
225 g/$\frac{1}{2}$ lb minced veal
250 g/$\frac{1}{2}$ lb lean minced lamb
3 medium-sized onions, chopped
2 garlic cloves, finely chopped
2 egg yolks
25 g/1 oz coarsely chopped fresh parsley
$\frac{1}{2}$ tsp ground white pepper
3 tbsp tomato purée
1$\frac{1}{2}$ tsp salt
2 large carrots, very finely chopped
225 ml/8 fl oz apple sauce
80 g/3 oz sultanas
4 tbsp apricot preserves
500 ml/16 fl oz tomato sauce
5 tomatoes, deseeded and mashed
3 tbsp brown sugar
2 tbsp white wine vinegar
$\frac{1}{2}$ tsp black pepper

Remove and discard the tough outer cabbage leaves. With a sharp knife, core the cabbage. Cook the cabbage in a large pot of boiling water with $\frac{1}{2}$ teaspoon of the salt for 5 minutes. Remove the cabbage and peel off all the outer leaves that will come away easily without tearing. Return the cabbage to the boiling water, remove after another 5 minutes and repeat the process of removing softened cabbage leaves. Finely dice any remaining cabbage and set it aside for use in the sauce.

♦ In a large mixing bowl, combine the minced sirloin, veal, and lamb. Add one of the chopped onions, the garlic, egg yolks, half of the chopped parsley, the white pepper, tomato purée and $\frac{1}{2}$ teaspoon salt. Mix the stuffing thoroughly.

♦ To make the sauce, combine the remaining salt, onions and parsley, the diced cabbage leaves, and the carrots, apple sauce, sultanas, apricot preserves, tomato sauce, tomatoes, brown sugar, vinegar and black pepper in a medium-sized saucepan. Stir over a low heat until well blended. Cover and simmer for 10 minutes over a very low heat.

♦ Place 2 tablespoons of the stuffing in the centre of each softened cabbage leaf. Bring the end of the cabbage leaf towards the centre, and then roll it over. Fold the cabbage leaf ends under so that the cabbage package is completely sealed. Repeat until all the cabbage leaves are stuffed and rolled. Save any remaining stuffing to add to the sauce.

♦ Preheat the oven to 180°C/350°F/Gas 4. Place the cabbage rolls side-by-side in 2 layers in a large saucepan. Pour the sauce, including any leftover stuffing, over the cabbage rolls. Cover and bake for 2 hours.

Holiday Carrots

SERVES 8

In addition to being traditional on Succoth, this dish is also often served on Purim.

700 g/1½ lb baby carrots, cut into small pieces
225 g/8 oz tinned mandarin orange sections, drained
60 ml/2 fl oz water
25 g/1 oz margarine
60 ml/2 fl oz fresh lime juice
¼ tsp salt

Place all the ingredients in a large wooden chopping bowl. Chop finely.
♦ Put the mixture into a medium-sized saucepan and simmer over a low heat for 20 minutes. Serve hot.

Berry Kuchen

SERVES 8

Borrowed from the German-Austrian Jews, this festive dessert is a delicious way to end a meal.

225 g/8 oz flour
½ tsp salt
175 g/6 oz unsalted margarine
2 tbsp lemon juice
40 g/1½ oz castor sugar
½ tsp vanilla essence
¼ tsp ground cinnamon
225 g/8 oz fresh or frozen blueberries or bilberries
225 g/8 oz fresh or frozen strawberries
225 g/8 oz fresh or frozen raspberries

If using frozen berries, thaw them completely and drain well.
♦ Preheat the oven to 190°C/375°F/Gas 5. In a large mixing bowl combine the flour, salt, margarine and lemon juice. Mix until the dough has an even consistency.
♦ Spread the dough mixture evenly in a 30 cm/12 in square baking dish.
♦ Combine the sugar, vanilla essence, berries and cinnamon in a mixing bowl. Mix well. Spoon the berry mixture into the baking dish on top of the dough. Bake for 1 hour 10 minutes. Serve warm.

*Russian Egg Drop Soup was traditionally served as
part of a Russian Sabbath Dinner (page 61).*

Kasha ABOVE LEFT *is a traditional Russian dish*
made with buckwheat groats, mushrooms and
onions (page 64).

♦

Braised Carrots ABOVE RIGHT *symbolized good luck*
at a Russian Chanuka Dinner (page 70).

♦

Merchant's Spiced Potatoes BELOW *is a Russian*
dish with strong Eastern influences (page 75).

Moscow Borscht ABOVE is a variation of the most
famous of all Russian dishes (page 77).

♦

Baked Apples BELOW provide a light finish to a
Polish Yom Kippur Dinner (page 83).

Chicken in the Pot with Soup ABOVE *is served with Kreplach and Matzoh Balls at a Polish Yom Kippur Dinner (page 83).*

♦

Garlic Chicken Soup ABOVE (OPPOSITE) *is a Polish country soup dating back to the 17th century (page 85).*

♦

Scholar's Vegetable Soup BELOW (OPPOSITE) *is thought to have been favoured by Talmudic scholars (page 98).*

Polish Herring Salad ABOVE OPPOSITE combines the
piquancy of herrings with the sweetness of pears (page 99).

♦

Lesco ABOVE is a traditional Hungarian
first course (page 102).

♦

Cold Cherry Soup BELOW (OPPOSITE) is an unusual
Hungarian soup (page 102).

New Potatoes with Wine ABOVE LEFT *makes a
delicious accompaniment to Beef Goulash
(page 104).*

◆

Kohlrabi Chicken Soup ABOVE RIGHT *is a
traditional first course at a Hungarian Holiday
Supper (page 107).*

◆

Chicken Paprikash BELOW *is a perfect centrepiece
for a Hungarian Holiday Dinner (page 107).*

Polish Dairy Lunch

*This menu is assembled from an assortment of favourite dishes from the
Jews of Cracow and Warsaw.*

Dairy Chopped Liver
Scholar's Vegetable Soup
Polish Herring Salad
Kasha Varneshkes
Carrot Cake
Pear Pie

Dairy 'Chopped Liver'
SERVES 6

The search for the perfect meatless substitute for chopped liver to be served at dairy meals has continued for the last 150 years. The recipe below is a very acceptable version, but as experienced Jewish cooks know, the search for the ultimate recipe goes on.

175 g/6 oz chickpeas, cooked and drained

175 g/6 oz red kidney beans, cooked and drained

1 hard-boiled egg, finely chopped

125 g/4 oz tinned mackerel fillets in tomato sauce

80 g/3 oz finely chopped onion

4 tbsp finely chopped celery

4 tbsp slivered carrot

2 tbsp lemon juice

1 tbsp red wine

Combine all the ingredients in a large wooden chopping bowl. Mash them into a paste with a fine and even consistency.
♦ Spoon the mixture into a serving bowl. Cover and chill for at least 2 hours. Serve with biscuits, black bread or on a bed of lettuce.

Scholar's Vegetable Soup
SERVES 6 — 8

Legend has it that Talmudic scholars, who wanted a pure diet and abstained from meat, favoured this traditional Polish-Jewish vegetable soup.

450 g/1 lb ripe tomatoes, seeded and finely chopped

4 large carrots, peeled and quartered

250 g/9 oz chopped celery

3 leeks, cut into sections

175 g/6 oz fresh green peas

125 g/4 oz dried lentils

1 tsp salt

1 small head cauliflower, cut into florets

1 bay leaf

$\frac{1}{2}$ tsp black pepper

1 tbsp diced green pepper

2.5 L/$4\frac{1}{2}$ pt water

1 large Spanish onion, halved

1.1 L/2 pt vegetable stock

Combine all the ingredients in a large soup pot. Bring to a boil, reduce the heat to medium and simmer for 3 hours, stirring occasionally. Serve in large soup bowls.

Polish Herring Salad

SERVES 6—8

This piquant salad features the addition of pear sections. Herring is something of a treat for Westernized Jews today, but at one time it was an every-day food, especially among the poor.

450 g/1 lb beetroot, cooked and diced

350 g/¾ lb new potatoes, cooked and diced

350 g/1 lb tinned pear sections, drained and cut into small pieces

900 g/32 oz bottled herring pieces, drained

350 g/12 oz finely diced onion

225 ml/8 fl oz red wine vinegar

½ tsp black pepper

¼ tsp salt

125 g/4 oz quartered mushrooms

450 ml/¾ pt soured cream

125 ml/4 fl oz white wine

Toss all the ingredients together in a large mixing bowl. Cover and chill for at least 3 hours before serving.

Kasha Varneshkes

SERVES 6

Kasha is a staple food throughout Russia and the Slavic countries. The variations are endless. Only use bow-tie pasta shapes; any other pasta shape won't taste right. The dish will still be authentic (perhaps more so) if 50 g/2 oz of sliced mushrooms are added with the onions.

125 g/4 oz medium-grain kasha(buckwheat groats)

1 egg

50 g/2 oz margarine or chicken fat

2 onions, diced

450 ml/¾ pt boiling water

salt to taste

225 g/8 oz pasta bow-ties

Beat the egg in a bowl and add the kasha. Stir well to coat the kasha.

♦ Heat a large heavy pan on top of the cooker. Add the kasha and cook, stirring, until each kasha grain is dry and separate. Make sure this is done thoroughly or the kasha will be soggy and lumpy.

♦ Melt 1 tablespoon of the margarine in a small frying pan. Add the onions and fry until soft.

♦ Add the onions, boiling water, remaining margarine and salt to taste to the kasha. Cover tightly and cook over a medium heat until all the water has been absorbed, about 40 minutes.

♦ Cook the pasta in a large pot of boiling water until it is cooked *al dente*. Drain well. Mix the pasta with the kasha and serve.

Carrot Cake

MAKES 1 CAKE

In Warsaw just before World War I, this cake was a favourite among café-goers seeking to emulate their Parisian counterparts.

350 g/12 oz flour

700 g/1½ lb sugar

3 tsp bicarbonate of soda

2 tsp ground cinnamon

1 tsp vanilla essence

350 ml/12 fl oz vegetable oil

6 eggs

5 carrots, finely grated

½ tsp salt

150 g/5 oz sultanas

50 g/2 oz slivered apple

Preheat the oven to 180°C/350°F/Gas 4. Mix all the ingredients together in a large mixing bowl until the consistency is even.

♦ Grease a 23 × 38cm/9 × 15in rectangular cake tin and pour in the batter. Bake for 40 minutes, or until a cocktail stick inserted into the centre of the cake comes out dry.

Pear Pie

SERVES 6—8

Pears are a favourite fruit in Eastern Europe.

225 g/8 oz shortcrust pastry

5 tbsp castor sugar

1 tbsp plain flour

1 tsp nutmeg

6 ripe pears, peeled, cored and sliced

1 tsp grated orange rind

4 tbsp chopped sultanas

2 tbsp lemon juice

2 tbsp sweet white wine

2 tbsp vegetable oil

125 ml/4 fl oz double cream

Preheat the oven to 200°C/400°F/Gas 6.

♦ Line a 23 cm/9 in pie tin with the pastry. Prick the pastry with a fork and sprinkle it with 2 tablespoons of the sugar, flour and nutmeg. Arrange the pear slices in the pastry case and sprinkle them with the orange rind and chopped sultanas. Combine the lemon juice, wine and vegetable oil in a bowl and mix well. Pour the mixture over the pear slices.

♦ Put the remaining sugar and cream in a bowl. Stir until all the sugar is dissolved. Pour the mixture over the pear slices.

♦ Bake the pie for 12 minutes. Reduce the heat to 180°C/350°F/Gas 4 and bake for 25 minutes. Serve warm.

Hungarian Jewish Supper

This meal of traditional Hungarian dishes is built around a main course of beef goulash, a staple of Hungarian cuisine.

Lesco
Cold Cherry Soup
Beef Goulash
Asparagus with Nutmeg
New Potatoes with Wine
Walnut Apricot Pancakes

◆

Lesco

SERVES 6—8

This traditional Hungarian starter is similar to a ragoût.

5 tbsp chicken fat

175 g/6 oz finely chopped onion

2 garlic cloves, chopped

900 g/2 lb ripe tomatoes, skinned, seeded and coarsely chopped

700 g/1½ lb green peppers, seeded and cut into strips

½ tsp salt

1 tsp black pepper

3 tbsp sweet Hungarian paprika

4 tbsp black olives, stoned and diced

225 ml/8 fl oz tomato purée

700 g/1½ lb kosher beef sausage, thinly sliced

6—8 eggs

Melt the chicken fat in a large saucepan. Add the onions and garlic and cook for 10—12 minutes over a low heat.

♦ Add the tomatoes, green peppers, salt, pepper, paprika and olives. Turn the heat up to medium, cover, and cook for 15 minutes.

♦ Add the tomato purée and sausage. Reduce the heat to low and simmer the lesco, covered, for 30 minutes.

♦ After the lesco has cooked for 25 minutes, fry the eggs on both sides until the whites are firm. Serve the lesco in soup bowls, topping each portion with a fried egg.

Cold Cherry Soup

SERVES 8

This unusual soup is made using both sour and black cherries and is served cold.

1 L/1¾ pt cold water

350 g/12 oz sugar

¼ tsp ground cinnamon

700 g/1½ lb fresh or tinned sour red cherries, stoned

700 g/1½ lb fresh or tinned black cherries, stoned

2 tbsp lemon juice

225 ml/8 fl oz red wine

¼ tsp dried dill

¼ tsp ground white pepper

2 tbsp water, at room temperature

1 tbsp arrowroot

In a medium-sized saucepan, combine all the ingredients except the tepid water and arrowroot. Bring to a boil over a medium heat. Partially cover the saucepan and reduce the heat to low. Simmer for 1 hour.

♦ In a small bowl, combine the arrowroot and tepid water. Stir well. Stir the mixture into the soup and turn the heat up to medium. Continue stirring until the soup begins to bubble. Reduce the heat to low. Simmer the soup, uncovered, for 2 minutes. Pour the soup into a glass bowl and chill for 1 hour. Serve cold.

Beef Goulash

SERVES 8

There is perhaps no dish so readily identified with Hungary as goulash. There are at least 80 standard variations calling for a variety of different ingredients. Below is a traditional beef goulash recipe.

1.8 kg/4lb lean beef sirloin, cut into small pieces

70 g/2½ oz margarine

1 large onion, coarsely chopped

1 medium-sized green pepper, seeded and finely diced

750 ml/1¼ pt beef stock

2 tbsp flour

1 large tomato, peeled, seeded and coarsely chopped

3 tbsp poppy seeds

2 tbsp Hungarian sweet paprika

60 ml/2 fl oz dry red wine

450 g/1 lb egg noodles

Melt the margarine in a large saucepan over a low heat. Add the onion, tomato and green pepper and fry for 5 minutes.
♦ Add the beef, paprika, red wine, beef stock, flour and poppy seeds. Simmer for 30 minutes. Add 225 ml/8 fl oz water, cover, and simmer for 90 minutes.
♦ While the goulash simmers, cook the egg noodles in a large pan of boiling water. Drain well. Serve the goulash on a bed of noodles.

Asparagus with Nutmeg

SERVES 8

The addition of nutmeg to this simple asparagus dish gives it a surprising flavour.

125 g/4 oz margarine

2 garlic cloves, quartered

1 tsp grated nutmeg

1 tbsp finely chopped onion

900 g/2 lb fresh asparagus, trimmed

Preheat the oven to 190°C/375°F/Gas 5. In a small saucepan, melt the margarine over a low heat. Add the garlic, nutmeg and onion.
♦ Place the asparagus in a large baking dish. Pour the margarine mixture over the asparagus and bake for 18 minutes. Serve hot.

New Potatoes with Wine

SERVES 6—8

New potatoes are delicious served this way. If medium-hot paprika is not available,
use sweet paprika and add ¼ teaspoon cayenne pepper.

1.1 kg/2½ lb new potatoes, quartered
450 ml/¾ pt white wine
1 garlic clove, halved
1 tsp medium-hot Hungarian paprika

Cook the new potatoes in a large pot of boiling water until tender, about 25 to 30 minutes.
♦ Drain the potatoes well and return them to the saucepan. Add the wine, garlic and paprika. Simmer over a low heat for 20 minutes. Serve hot.

Walnut Apricot Pancakes

SERVES 8

Quite similar to French crêpes, this traditional Hungarian dessert will satisfy any
sweet tooth.

4 eggs
300 ml/½ pt water
125 ml/4 fl oz soda water
225 g/8 oz sifted flour
6 tbsp sugar
½ tsp salt
2 tsp vanilla essence
450 g/1 lb apricot preserves
4 tbsp strawberry preserves
125 g/4 oz finely chopped walnuts
125 g/4 oz margarine
4 tbsp fine brown sugar

In a medium-sized mixing bowl beat the eggs. Add the soda water, salt and vanilla essence. Mix well. Fold in the flour and sugar. Stir until the batter has an even consistency.
♦ Combine the apricot preserves, strawberry preserves and chopped walnuts in a bowl. Mix well.
♦ For each pancake, melt 1 teaspoon of the margarine in a small frying pan over a medium heat. Pour a thin layer of batter into the pan. Cook the pancake for 2—3 minutes. Turn the pancake and cook for 1 minute.
♦ Fill each pancake with 3 teaspoons of the preserves and nut mixture. Roll each pancake into a cylinder and place it in a baking dish in a slow oven to keep warm. Sprinkle each pancake with brown sugar before serving. Serve warm.

Hungarian Jewish Holiday Supper

Any holiday, religious or secular, could prompt this extensive menu of Hungarian specialities.

Sautéed Chicken Livers
Stuffed Sauerkraut
Kohlrabi Chicken Soup
Chicken Paprikash
Carrot Dumplings
Peaches in Red Wine

Sautéed Chicken Livers

SERVES 8

Featuring two different kinds of wine, this recipe has a decidedly Continental flavour.

4 tbsp chicken fat

700 g/1½ lb fresh chicken livers

225 ml/8 fl oz white wine

60 ml/2 fl oz dry sherry

1 tbsp chopped parsley

1 tbsp finely chopped onion

1 garlic clove, finely chopped

1 small shallot, finely chopped

¼ tsp salt

¼ tsp ground white pepper

Melt the chicken fat in a large frying pan over a low heat. Add the chicken livers and fry until browned, about 5 minutes. Add the remaining ingredients, raise the heat to medium, cover and cook for 5 minutes.

◆ Remove the cover and cook until the liquid is almost gone, stirring occasionally. Serve with biscuits or crusty bread.

Stuffed Sauerkraut

SERVES 8

This is the Hungarian version of stuffed cabbage. It is unique in that the sauce is neither red nor sweet.

10 large white cabbage leaves

4 tbsp chicken fat

900 g/2 lb minced veal

150 g/5 oz cooked rice

3 garlic cloves, quartered

175 g/6 oz finely chopped onion

¼ tsp salt

¼ tsp white pepper

1 tsp Hungarian sweet paprika

Cook the cabbage leaves in a large pan of boiling water for 5 to 8 minutes or until they are soft. Drain well and set aside.

◆ In a large saucepan, melt the chicken fat. Add the minced veal, rice, garlic, onions, salt and pepper. Cook over a low heat, stirring often, until the veal loses its raw look. Cover and simmer for 20 minutes, stirring frequently.

◆ Add the sauerkraut and paprika to the veal mixture and cook, stirring frequently, for 2 minutes.

◆ Spoon 3 tablespoons of the veal mixture on to the centre of each cabbage leaf. Roll up the cabbage leaves, tucking in the edges of the leaves as you roll.

◆ Place the cabbage rolls in a large saucepan. Add 225 ml/8 fl oz of cold water and cover. Simmer over a low heat for 50 minutes. Serve warm.

Kohlrabi Chicken Soup

SERVES 8

No cuisine makes more use of kohlrabi, a rather obscure root vegetable, than the Hungarian. Fresh kohlrabi can be purchased at most well-stocked markets.

1.4 kg/3 lb chicken, cut into pieces

3 medium onions, halved

1.75 L/3¼ pt chicken stock

1 leek

½ tsp salt

¼ tsp black pepper

450-600 g/1-1¼ lb fresh kohlrabi, peeled and cut into small pieces

8 tbsp coarsely chopped fresh parsley

3 tbsp margarine

60 ml/2 fl oz white wine

Place the chicken, onions, chicken stock, leek, salt and pepper in a large soup pot. Simmer, covered, over a medium heat for 50 minutes. Add the kohlrabi, parsley, margarine and wine. Simmer, covered, for an additional 35 minutes.
♦ Remove the chicken and use it in another dish. Serve the soup hot.

Chicken Paprikash

SERVES 6—8

This delectable chicken dish is the perfect centrepiece for a Hungarian holiday dinner. Although most cookery books suggest serving it with egg noodles, for true authenticity it should be served on a bed of rice.

1.8 kg/4 lb chicken, cut into pieces

225 g/8 oz margarine

175 g/6 oz grated carrots

70 g/2½ oz chopped onions

3 garlic cloves, quartered

50 g/2 oz flour

4 tsp Hungarian sweet paprika

¼ tsp salt

¼ tsp black pepper

125 ml/4 fl oz red wine

900 ml/1½ pt chicken stock

Place all the ingredients except for 450 ml/¾ pt of the chicken stock in a large soup pot. Simmer, covered, over a low heat for 1 hour.
♦ Add the remaining chicken stock, reduce the heat to very low and simmer covered, for 1 hour longer. Serve on a bed or rice.

Carrot Dumplings

SERVES 6—8

In the days when refined white sugar was scarce and expensive, sweet dishes were often made with naturally sweet carrots. These carrot dumplings are both sweet and hearty.

10 large carrots, peeled and finely shredded

1 large sweet potato, cooked, peeled and mashed

4 tbsp chicken fat

4 tbsp potato flour

$\frac{1}{4}$ tsp salt

225 ml/8 fl oz water

125 g/4 oz margarine

1 large onion, finely diced

Cook the carrots in a saucepan of boiling water until tender, about 8 to 10 minutes. Drain well.

♦ Combine the carrots and mashed sweet potato in a large mixing bowl. Mash together until the consistency is even. Shape the mixture into thick, round cakes.

♦ Melt the chicken fat in a large frying pan. Add the potato flour and brown it. Add the carrot dumpling cakes and water. Cover the pan and lower the heat. Steam the dumplings for 3 to 5 minutes. Remove the dumplings from the pan and drain them on kitchen paper.

♦ In a small saucepan, melt the margarine. Add the onion and salt. Simmer for 5 minutes over a very low heat.

♦ Pour the margarine mixture over the carrot dumplings before serving.

Peaches in Red Wine

SERVES 6—8

This dish makes a refreshing end to a substantial meal.

450 ml/$\frac{3}{4}$ pt red wine

1 tbsp currant preserves

1 tbsp sugar

700 g/1$\frac{1}{2}$ lb tinned peaches, drained

In a medium-sized mixing bowl, combine the wine, preserves and sugar. Stir with a fork until the consistency is even and any lumps are dissolved. Add the peaches. Chill for at least 1 hour before serving.

Romanian Jewish Dinner

This menu is a sampling of traditional Romanian cuisine. Some dishes, such as the nearly flourless walnut torte, are Jewish in origin. Others, like mamaliga, are classic Romanian dishes enjoyed by Jews and Gentiles alike.

Sour Soup

Mamaliga

Stuffed Beef Hearts

Walnut Torte

Sour Soup

SERVES 8

Found only in Romania, this unusual soup gets its savoury flavour from the veal.

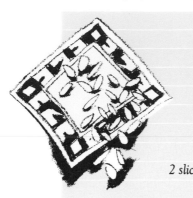

1 tbsp olive oil

1 large carrot, finely chopped

4 tbsp chopped celery

2 onions, diced

350 ml/12 fl oz water

4 tbsp chopped parsley

1 L/1¾ pt sauerkraut juice

2 beaten eggs

2 slices bread, soaked in water and drained

½ tsp salt

¼ tsp black pepper

15 g/1½ oz cooked rice

½ tsp chopped fresh dill

700 g/1½ lb minced veal

Heat the olive oil in a large saucepan over a medium heat. Add the carrots, celery and onions and fry for 8 minutes, stirring frequently. Add the water and parsley to the saucepan and bring to a boil. Cook for 1 minute. Add the sauerkraut juice and reduce the heat slightly. Cook for 15 minutes.

♦ In a large mixing bowl, combine the eggs, bread, salt, pepper, rice, dill and veal. Mix with a fork until the consistency is even. Form the veal mixture into balls approximately 2.5 cm/1 in in diameter. Drop the meatballs into the simmering soup and reduce the heat to low. Simmer for 40 minutes and serve.

Mamaliga

SERVES 6—8

Mamaliga is a staple food in Romania.

200 g/7 oz corn meal

1½ tbsp chicken fat

450 ml/¾ pt boiling water

½ tsp salt

¼ tsp black pepper

2 eggs, separated

450 ml/¾ pt buttermilk

1¼ tsp bicarbonate of soda

4 tbsp melted margarine

In a large pot, combine the corn meal with the chicken fat and boiling water. Mix until the consistency of the dough is even. Add the salt, pepper, egg yolks, buttermilk and bicarbonate of soda. Combine thoroughly.

♦ Beat the egg whites until they are stiff. Fold them into the corn meal mixture.

♦ Grease a large casserole dish with 1 tablespoon of the melted margarine. Preheat the oven to 170°C/325°F/Gas 5. Scrape the corn meal mixture into the casserole with a rubber scraper. Bake for 1 hour 15 minutes. Pour the remaining melted margarine over the mamaliga before serving.

Stuffed Beef Hearts

SERVES 8

The Romanian Jews perfected the difficult art of preparing offal, as this dish illustrates.

2 beef hearts, prepared for stuffing

4 tbsp olive oil

3 garlic cloves, finely chopped

4 tbsp chopped fresh parsley

50 g/2 oz diced mushrooms

80 g/3 oz sultanas

80 g/3 oz dried apricots

2 hard-boiled eggs, finely chopped

125 ml/4 fl oz vegetable oil

750 ml/1¼ pt tomato sauce

2 tbsp tomato purée

Coat the beef hearts inside and out with the olive oil. In a large mixing bowl, combine the garlic, parsley, mushrooms, sultanas, apricots and eggs thoroughly.
♦ Stuff the beef hearts with the mixture. Tie the hearts closed with kitchen string.
♦ Heat the vegetable oil in a large saucepan over a medium heat. Add the beef hearts and brown on all sides. Add the tomato sauce and tomato purée. Cover and simmer for 90 minutes over a low heat. Split the hearts in half and serve.

Walnut Torte

SERVES 8

An ingenious invention of the Romanian Jews, imitating their Viennese relatives.

450 g/1 lb shelled walnut halves

70 g/2½ oz unsalted margarine

½ tbsp flour

5 eggs, at room temperature, separated

125 g/4 oz sugar

1 tsp vanilla essence

350 g/12 oz peach preserves

1 tbsp cocoa powder

125 g/4 oz plain chocolate, crumbled

1 tbsp boiling water

Preheat the oven to 180°C/350°F/Gas 4. Spread the walnuts in a single layer in a large baking tin and roast them for 12 to 15 minutes. Chop the walnuts finely.
♦ Grease a 23 × 7.5 cm/9 × 3 in baking dish with ½ tablespoon margarine. Dust the pan with the flour.
♦ In a large mixing bowl, gradually combine the egg yolks with the sugar, beating constantly until the egg yolks are lemon-coloured. Stir in the vanilla essence.
♦ In another bowl, beat the egg whites until they are stiff. Gradually beat the walnuts into the egg whites. Gently fold the egg whites into the egg yolk mixture. Scrape the batter into the greased baking dish. Bake for 25 minutes.
♦ Invert the baking dish over a cooling rack, remove the dish, and leave to cool.
♦ Heat the peach preserves until they are warm. Spread them on the cake.
♦ Melt the cocoa and chocolate over a low heat, gradually adding the margarine.
♦ Spread the chocolate icing over the cake. Chill for 1 hour before serving.

Yugoslav Jewish Supper

*Although the cuisines of Yugoslavia and Czechoslovakia are hearty and
pleasing, they do not have a large repertoire of desserts. Most meals end
with fresh fruit in season, a plain cake or perhaps some home-made
preserves. This simple four-course supper is guaranteed to fill the
hungriest stomach.*

Vegetable Caviar
Aubergine Soup
Yugoslavian Leg of Lamb
Serbian Apple Cake

Vegetable Caviar

SERVES 6—8

Serve this delectable vegetarian dish in exactly the same way as real caviar — by itself, accompanied by thin slices of black bread and perhaps a squeeze of lemon.

1 small aubergine, peeled
1 small marrow, halved and seeded
3 large green peppers, seeded
$\frac{1}{2}$ tsp salt
$\frac{1}{2}$ tsp black pepper
$\frac{1}{2}$ tsp finely chopped garlic
3 tbsp lemon juice
6 tbsp vegetable oil
3 tbsp finely chopped fresh parsley

Preheat the oven to 240°C/475°F/Gas 9. Place the aubergine, marrow and green peppers in a baking dish. Bake for 30 minutes and remove the peppers. Bake the marrow and aubergine for 15 minutes longer.

♦ Cut the peppers into strips. Cut the aubergine into cubes. Scoop the pulp from the marrow and discard the skin.

♦ Combine the aubergine, peppers and marrow in a medium-sized mixing bowl. Chop and mix thoroughly until the mixture is well combined. Add the salt, black pepper, garlic, lemon juice, vegetable oil and parsley. Blend thoroughly. Chill for at least 2 hours before serving.

Aubergine Soup

SERVES 6—8

This unusual soup shows a touch of Turkish influence.

125 ml/4 fl oz olive oil
125 g/4 oz mushrooms, quartered
1 large onion, coarsely chopped
1 large tomato, cut into eighths
1 large aubergine, peeled and diced
450 ml/$\frac{3}{4}$ pt beef stock
$\frac{1}{2}$ tsp dried parsley
$\frac{1}{4}$ tsp salt
$\frac{1}{4}$ tsp white pepper
$\frac{1}{4}$ tsp dried thyme
$\frac{1}{4}$ tsp dried marjoram
$\frac{1}{4}$ tsp grated nutmeg

Heat the olive oil in a large pot over a low heat. Add the mushrooms, onion and tomato and fry for 10 minutes.

♦ Add the remaining ingredients to the pot. Cover and simmer for 35 to 40 minutes. Serve hot.

Yugoslavian Leg of Lamb

SERVES 6—8

Use the best leg of lamb you can find for this traditional Passover dish.

3-3.5 kg/7-8 lb leg of lamb, boned and tied
1 tsp salt
225 ml/8 fl oz red wine vinegar
3 bay leaves
450 ml/¾ pt water
350 g/12 oz diced onions
4 tbsp coarsely chopped fresh parsley
½ tsp dried thyme
½ tsp black pepper
4 large tomatoes, coarsely chopped
2 tbsp chicken fat

Rub the leg of lamb with the salt. Put the lamb in a large casserole.

♦ In a small saucepan combine the bay leaves, vinegar, water, onions, parsley, thyme, pepper and tomatoes. Bring the liquid to a boil over a high heat. Cook for 1 minute and remove the saucepan from the heat. Cool the mixture to room temperature and pour it over the lamb. Leave the lamb to marinate in the refrigerator for 6 hours, uncovered. Turn the lamb every 1½ hours.

♦ Preheat the oven to 190°C/375°F/Gas 5. Melt the chicken fat in a small saucepan over a medium heat. Remove the lamb from the refrigerator. Pour the chicken fat over the lamb. Roast the lamb for 2 hours, basting every 30 minutes. If the liquid in the casserole starts to boil too fast, reduce the heat to 180°C/350°F/Gas 4. Save the pan drippings for gravy.

Serbian Apple Cake

SERVES 6—8

In the days of the Austro-Hungarian empire, Yugoslavia was called Serbia.

150 g/5 oz margarine
200 g/7 oz sugar
2 eggs, separated
2 tbsp fresh lemon juice
225 g/8 oz flour
2 tbsp ground almonds
2 tsp baking powder
½ tsp salt
¼ tsp grated nutmeg
4 apples, peeled, cored and thinly sliced

Preheat the oven to 180°C/350°F/Gas 4. Beat the margarine until creamy. Add 150 g/5 oz of the sugar and continue beating until the mixture is fluffy. Beat in the egg yolks, one at a time. Beat in the lemon juice.

♦ In another mixing bowl, beat the egg whites until they are stiff.

♦ In another bowl sift together the flour, almonds, baking powder, salt and nutmeg.

♦ Alternately add the egg white and flour mixtures to the batter, beating after each addition. Pour the batter into a 23 cm/9 in deep cake tin with spring clip. Press the apple slices into the top of the batter. Sprinkle the cake with the rest of the sugar and bake for 50 minutes. Allow the cake to cool for 10 minutes before serving.

Yugoslav Jewish Dinner

This dinner incorporates two Yugoslavian specialities. The braised chicken dish is descended from the preparation of sacrificed doves in the Temple in ancient times. Slatko, or Yugoslavian preserves, is a proper ending to any Yugoslavian meal.

Celery Chicken Soup
Braised Chicken
Yugoslavian Endive
Watermelon Slatko
Strawberry Plum Slatko

Celery Chicken Soup

SERVES 6—8

This Balkan variation on chicken soup used celeriac for its distinct flavour.

1.5 L/2½ pt chicken stock
2 large celeriac, peeled and sliced
50 g/2 oz coarsely chopped celery
50 g /2 oz chopped leeks
1 small chicory, chopped
2 large carrots, diced
½ tsp salt
½ tsp white pepper

In a large soup pot, bring the chicken stock to a boil. Add the remaining ingredients, reduce the heat to low and simmer for 40 minutes. Serve hot.

Braised Chicken

SERVES 6—8

This dish is traditionally made with pigeon or game birds. Small chickens or guinea fowl can be used instead.

3 small chickens, split
6 tbsp olive oil
50 g/2 oz margarine
2 garlic cloves, quartered
2 onions, coarsely chopped
225 g/8 oz mushrooms, quartered
2 tbsp lemon juice
450 ml/¾ pt white wine
2 tbsp chopped parsley
½ tsp dried sage
¼ tsp dried marjoram
½ tsp salt
½ tsp black pepper

Put the chickens, skin-side up, into a very large saucepan or 2 smaller ones. Pour the olive oil over the chickens.

◆ In a small saucepan, melt the margarine. Add the garlic, onions and mushrooms. Fry over a low heat for 3 to 5 minutes. Add the lemon juice, wine, parsley, sage, marjoram, salt and pepper and stir well. Pour the mixture evenly over the chickens. Cover and simmer over a medium heat for 15 minutes. Reduce the heat to low and simmer for 45 minutes or until the chickens are tender. Add more wine during the cooking if needed.

Yugoslavian Endive

SERVES 6—8

The endive that we enjoy in salads can also be served as a delicious hot vegetable.

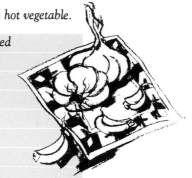

> 1 large head curly endive, trimmed and coarsely chopped
> 1 large tomato, cut into eighths
> 4 garlic cloves, halved
> 1 small onion, finely chopped
> $\frac{1}{2}$ tsp salt
> $\frac{1}{2}$ tsp black pepper
> 450 ml/$\frac{3}{4}$ pt water
> 4 tbsp olive oil

Place all the ingredients into a medium-sized saucepan. Cover the saucepan and simmer over a medium heat for 15 minutes. Reduce the heat to low and simmer for 20 minutes longer. Serve hot.

Watermelon Slatko

MAKES 1.5L/2$\frac{1}{2}$ PT

Watermelon preserve should be served with Strawberry Plum Slatko in silver dishes.

> 900 g/2 lb watermelon rind, all pink flesh removed
> 1 tsp vanilla essence
> 4 tbsp lemon juice
> 900 g/2 lb sugar

With a sharp knife, remove the green outer skin from the watermelon rind. Cut the rind into small cubes. Place the watermelon rind cubes into a 2.5 L/4$\frac{3}{4}$ pt saucepan. Add enough water to cover the rind cubes and bring the liquid to a boil. Cook for 1 minute and drain. Repeat the process with fresh water. Cover the rinds with water a third time and simmer over a low heat for 20 minutes. Drain well.
♦ Add 175 ml/6 fl oz water to the rind along with the vanilla essence and the lemon juice. Raise the heat to medium and gradually stir in the sugar. When all the sugar has dissolved, reduce the heat to low and simmer for 2 hours.
♦ Store in sterilized glass jars in the refrigerator.

Strawberry Plum Slatko

MAKES 950 ml/32 fl oz

Serve slatko with plain cakes or simple sugar cookies.

> 450 g/1 lb sugar
> 350 g/$\frac{3}{4}$ lb damsons or other ripe purple plums, stoned and quartered
> 225 g/$\frac{1}{2}$ lb fresh strawberries, quartered
> 3 tbsp lemon juice

Combine the sugar, plums and strawberries in a large saucepan. Stir well. Cover and cook over a medium heat for 10 minutes. Stir with a fork to make sure the sugar melts. Cook for a further 20 minutes or until the sugar is completely dissolved.
♦ Add the lemon juice and cook for 10 minutes longer. Remove the saucepan from the heat and leave the slatko to stand, covered, at room temperature for 12 hours.
♦ Store in sterilized glass jars in the refrigerator.

Mamaliga ABOVE (OPPOSITE) is a staple food in
Romania (page 110).

◆

Aubergine Soup ABOVE RIGHT (OPPOSITE) comes
from Yugoslavia (page 113).

◆

Yugoslavian Endive BELOW (OPPOSITE) goes well
with Braised Chicken (page 117).

◆

Slatko ABOVE is a traditional end to a Yugoslavian
meal (page 117).

CHAPTER THREE

Germany
and
Austria

The Jews have been part of the German-speaking world for the last thousand years. In the fourth century, Cologne had a large Jewish population. By the eleventh century, Jews were an integral part of the Germanic cultural and economic world. It was in Germany in the 1850s that the *Haskalah* or enlightenment movement began, which paved the way for the assimilation of German Jews. Three of the greatest thinkers of the late nineteenth and early twentieth century, Karl Marx, Sigmund Freud and Albert Einstein, were Jews. By the beginning of the twentieth century, Jews in Germany and Austria had become an influential force in general culture.

Nevertheless, the German-speaking Jews were always subject to fierce anti-Semitism. The culmination of this anti-Semitism came with the Holocaust of World War II. The Jewish population of Germany, over half a million before the war, was virtually destroyed. Today, about 30,000 Jews continue to live in Germany.

Jews have lived in Austria, and in particular Vienna, since Roman times. The first ghetto there was instituted in the thirteenth century, situated around the square today called *Judenplatz*. In the thirteenth and fourteenth centuries the Viennese Jewish community was recognized as one of the most important in Europe. Persecution in the fifteenth century led to a sharp drop in their numbers. The Jews returned slowly after 1675 and gradually became prominent again. In 1781 the Emperor Joseph II granted increased liberties to the Jews, anticipating the emancipation that came in the nineteenth century. In 1826 the *Stadttempel*, the main synagogue in Vienna and the only currently active one, was dedicated. At the end of the nineteenth century and during the first quarter of this century, Vienna was a centre of Zionism. Dr Theodore Herzl, the guiding force behind Zionism, lived and worked in Vienna. The Viennese Jews accomplished remarkable things during the golden age from 1848 to 1938. This thriving community of 180,000 was annihilated between 1939 and 1945, and the current population is about 10,000.

As the Jews became more and more integrated into the fabric of German life, so did their cooking. They were fond of sausages and wursts, and took their sauerbraten seriously. Herring salads were popular, as were compotes for dessert. German-Jewish baking was said to be lighter than that of the Gentiles because no lard was used in the dough.

Some of the most famous Jewish dishes come from Germany and Austria. Sadly the recipes have been preserved only by those who fled persecution.

Challah ABOVE is traditionally eaten on the
Sabbath. Its origins are very ancient (page 126).

♦

Green Beans Paprika BELOW is a staple dish of
Austrian Jewish cooking (page 131).

German Austrian Friday Night Dinner

This Friday night repast features a traditional roast stuffed chicken, a delicious German variation on stuffed cabbage, and a delicate purée of mixed vegetables, a German speciality.

Challah

Bean, Mushroom and Asparagus Purée

Traditional Roast Chicken

German Austrian Stuffed Cabbage

Sponge Cake with Brandy Sauce

♦

גרמניה ואוסטריה
Challah

MAKES 2 LOAVES

The origins of Challah, the twisted egg bread traditionally eaten on the Sabbath and holidays, are very ancient. In the days of the Temple, women would offer a portion of their bread dough, called the Challah, to the priests as a dedication to God. Challah recipes always make two loaves, and both loaves are traditionally placed on the table on Friday night. This is in commemoration of the double portion of manna the Israelites received on Friday as they wandered in the desert after fleeing Egypt.

225 ml/8 fl oz lukewarm water
50 g/2 oz active dry yeast
5 tsp sugar
700g/1½ lb flour
1½ tsp salt
3 eggs
60 ml/2 fl oz vegetable oil
1 egg yolk

In a small bowl combine the water, yeast and 1 teaspoon sugar. Leave it to stand for 3 minutes and then stir until the yeast is dissolved. Leave it for a further 5 minutes.
♦ Combine 450 g/1 lb of the flour with the salt and remaining sugar in a large, deep mixing bowl. Make a well in the centre of the flour and pour in the yeast mixture. Add the eggs and vegetable oil. Gently stir until the ingredients are blended together. Stirring more vigorously, blend in the remaining flour.
♦ Turn the dough out onto a lightly floured surface and knead for 20 minutes with a rolling pin, flattening the dough with the rolling pin, gathering it back into a ball and flattening again. Place the dough ball into a bowl, cover with a clean cloth, and leave it to stand for 45 minutes or until it is nearly doubled in bulk.
♦ Turn the dough out and knead for 5 minutes. Leave to rest for 5 minutes.
♦ Cut the dough in half with a sharp knife. Cut each half into thirds. Roll each piece of dough into a cylinder that tapers at each end. Pinch the ends of the 3 dough cylinders together. Braid the cylinders and pinch the other ends together. Repeat with the remaining dough. Place the challahs on a lightly greased baking sheet and leave them to stand for 30 minutes.
♦ Preheat the oven to 200°C/400°F/Gas 6. In a small bowl, beat the egg yolk with 2 tablespoons cold water. Brush the tops of the challahs with the egg yolk and bake for 20 minutes. Reduce the oven temperature to 190°C/375°F/Gas 5 and bake for 40 minutes longer, or until the challahs are lightly browned. Cool on a rack.

Bean, Mushroom and Asparagus Purée

SERVES 6

This dish is adapted to kosher requirements from the haute cuisine of Germany.

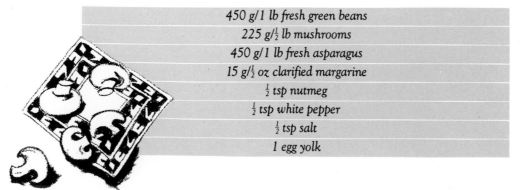

450 g/1 lb fresh green beans
225 g/½ lb mushrooms
450 g/1 lb fresh asparagus
15 g/½ oz clarified margarine
½ tsp nutmeg
½ tsp white pepper
½ tsp salt
1 egg yolk

Fill a large pot to the depth of 4 cm/1½ in with cold water. Add the green beans, mushrooms and asparagus. Cook over a low heat for 5 minutes. Add the clarified margarine, nutmeg, pepper and salt. Cook for a further 1 minute.

♦ Place the vegetables, along with the egg yolk and 125 ml/4 fl oz of the cooking liquid, in a liquidizer or food processor. Purée in bursts of 30 seconds until the vegetable mixture is smooth and well blended. Serve hot with croûtons.

Traditional Roast Chicken

SERVES 6

The hallmark of a German-Jewish Sabbath meal, this traditional dish is still a big favourite today.

1.5-1.8 kg/3½-4 lb roasting chicken, with liver
1 tsp salt
1 tbsp ground ginger
2 garlic cloves, finely chopped
1 tsp cayenne pepper
80 g/3 oz unflavoured soft breadcrumbs
50 g/2 oz chopped celery
50 g/2 oz chopped mushrooms
40 g/1½ oz shredded carrots
2 tbsp vegetable oil
1 tbsp chopped fresh parsley or 1 tsp dried parsley
½ tsp dried thyme
½ tsp dried marjoram
4 tbsp melted margarine
225 ml/8 fl oz boiling water
1.3 kg/3 lb potatoes, cut into sixths
3 large onions, cut into sixths

Preheat the oven to 180°C/350°F/Gas 4. Place the cleaned chicken on a greased roasting pan. Reserve the chicken liver. Sprinkle the skin with ½ teaspoon each of the salt, garlic, ginger and cayenne pepper. Roast the chicken for 30 minutes.

♦ While the chicken roasts, prepare the stuffing. In a mixing bowl combine the breadcrumbs with the celery, mushrooms, carrots, oil, and the remaining salt, garlic, ginger and cayenne pepper. Add the parsley, thyme and marjoram. Mix well.

♦ Put the chicken liver in a small saucepan and add enough cold water to cover. Bring to the boil and cook until the liver is done, about 10 minutes. Drain well. Chop the liver coarsely. Add the chopped liver to the stuffing mixture. Add the melted margarine and the boiling water. Mix well.

♦ Remove the chicken from the oven and fill the cavity with the stuffing. Arrange the potato and onion pieces around the chicken in the roasting pan. Return the chicken to the oven and roast for 1½ to 2 hours basting with the pan drippings every 30 minutes. Sprinkle the chicken, potatoes and onions with paprika after the final basting.

German Austrian Stuffed Cabbage

SERVES 6 TO 8

1 medium-sized green cabbage, cored
4 tbsp vegetable oil
2 large onions, chopped
275g/10 oz cooked rice
4 eggs, beaten
40g/1½ oz sultanas
½ tsp salt
1 tsp black pepper
25g/1 oz margarine
80 g/3 oz seedless green grapes, halved
50 g/2 oz shredded red cabbage
6 tinned tomatoes, chopped

Separate the leaves from the cabbage. Blanch the leaves in a large pot of boiling water for 5 minutes. Drain well.

♦ Heat half the oil in a frying pan. Add the onions and brown over a low heat. Add the rice, eggs and sultanas. Cook, stirring frequently, for 30 seconds. Add the salt, pepper, margarine and grapes. Cook, stirring frequently, for 90 seconds.

♦ Place 2 to 3 tablespoons of the rice filling at the edge of a cabbage leaf. Roll the leaf up, tucking the ends under. Repeat with the remaining cabbage leaves until the rice filling is used up. Coarsely chop the remaining cabbage leaves.

♦ Heat the remaining oil in a large frying pan over a moderate heat. Add the chopped green cabbage and the red cabbage. Fry for 3 to 4 minutes. Add the stuffed cabbage leaves and tomatoes. Cover and cook for 12 minutes.

Sponge Cake with Brandy Sauce

MAKES 1 CAKE

Sponge cake is a traditional dessert served on the Sabbath and holidays.

8 eggs, separated
450 g/1 lb sugar
275 g/10 oz sifted flour
½ tsp cream of tartar
3 tsp vanilla essence
125 ml/4 fl oz brandy
125 g/4 oz fresh or drained tinned cherries, stoned
125 g/4 oz drained tinned mandarin oranges
125 ml/4 fl oz orange juice

Preheat the oven to 150°C/300°F/Gas 2. In a large bowl, beat the egg whites until they are stiff but not dry. Beat in 350 g/12 oz of the sugar.

♦ In another bowl, beat the egg yolks with the remaining sugar. Add the egg yolks to the egg whites. Fold in the flour, cream of tartar, 2 teaspoons of the vanilla essence and 60 ml/2 fl oz of the brandy.

♦ Pour the batter into a greased 23-cm/9-in square baking tin. Bake for 70 minutes. Cool the cake in the tin.

♦ To make the brandy sauce, combine the remaining vanilla essence and brandy with the cherries, mandarin oranges and orange juice in a bowl. Mix well. Spoon the sauce over slices of the cake just before serving.

German Austrian Dairy Lunch

This elegant lunch begins with a savoury onion pudding. It features poached sole and the famous Viennese strudel. The green beans with paprika are a reminder of Vienna's history as a crossroads between eastern and western Europe.

Onion Pudding
Egg Salad
Poached Sole
Green Beans Paprika
Viennese Strudel

Onion Pudding

SERVES 6

A savoury treat and an unusual beginning for a classic German-Jewish luncheon, onion puddings were very popular among the Viennese Jews who invented the dish. Onion puddings also became standard in Polish-Jewish cooking.

50 g/2 oz butter
60 ml/2 fl oz white wine
½ tsp dried dill
2 garlic cloves, quartered
6 large onions, coarsely chopped
3 tbsp sugar
150 g/5 oz unflavoured breadcrumbs
125 g/4 oz crumbled matzoh
175 g/6 oz diced mild cheese

Melt 3 tablespoons of the butter in a large saucepan and add the wine, dill and garlic. Reduce the heat to low and add the onions and sugar. Stir gently until the sugar has completely dissolved. Simmer for another 5 minutes. Remove the saucepan from the heat.

♦ Preheat the oven to 190°C/375°F/Gas 5. Grease a 23-cm/9-in pie dish with the remaining butter. Spoon a thin layer of the onion mixture into the dish. Cover with a thin layer of the breadcrumbs and crumbled matzoh. Repeat the process until the onion, breadcrumbs and matzoh are used up.

♦ Top the pudding with the cheese and bake for 15 minutes, or until the cheese is melted and lightly browned. Remove the pudding from the oven, cut it into squares or wedges and serve hot.

Egg Salad

SERVES 6

This piquant version of egg salad is served as a starter, not as a sandwich filling.

6 hard-boiled eggs
4 tbsp mayonnaise
1 carrot, diced
1 large celery stalk, diced
1 small onion, finely chopped
2 tbsp chopped green pepper
1 large pimento, chopped
2 tbsp sweet pickle relish
1 tbsp Dijon-style mustard
½ tsp celery salt
1 tsp Worcestershire sauce
1 tsp cayenne pepper
1 tsp paprika

In a large mixing bowl, combine all the ingredients except the paprika. Mix roughly with a fork until the consistency, texture and colour of the mixture is even throughout.

♦ Arrange the egg salad on a bed of lettuce. Sprinkle with paprika. Chill for 10 minutes before serving.

גרמניה ואוסטריה

Poached Sole

SERVES 6

This method for poaching fresh fish was extremely popular among affluent German-Jewish families in the nineteenth century.

450 ml/$\frac{3}{4}$ pt dry vermouth

2 large onions, sliced

4 parsley sprigs

1 bay leaf

2 tbsp fresh basil leaves or 1 tsp dried basil

1 tbsp black pepper

150 g/5 oz chopped celery

1 L/1 $\frac{3}{4}$ pt water

1 tsp salt

1.8 kg/4 lb sole or plaice fillets

6 tomatoes

4 egg yolks, beaten

225 ml/8 fl oz double cream

To make the poaching liquid, combine the vermouth, onions, parsley, bay leaf, basil, black pepper, celery, water, thyme and salt in a large pot. Simmer over a low heat for 30 minutes.

♦ Arrange the fillets on a large square of muslin. Top with the tomatoes and wrap with the muslin.

♦ Pass the broth through a sieve into a fish poacher or large frying pan. Add the fish and tomatoes. Cover and simmer gently over a low heat for 10 minutes.

♦ Remove the fish and tomatoes from the poacher. Remove the muslin and arrange the fillets on a warm serving platter. Keep warm while you make the sauce.

♦ Whisk the egg yolks and cream into the remaining broth in the poacher. Cook over a medium heat, stirring constantly, for 5 minutes or until the sauce thickens. Do not let it boil. Pour the sauce over the fish and serve with lemon slices.

Green Beans Paprika

SERVES 6

This dish is a staple of Austrian-Jewish cooking with a strong Hungarian influence.

900 g/2 lb fresh green beans, trimmed and halved

125 g/4 oz butter

225 g/8 oz coarsely chopped spring onions

1 tbsp flour

450 ml/$\frac{3}{4}$ pt soured cream

1 tbsp sweet paprika

$\frac{1}{2}$ tsp salt

Cook the green beans in a large pot of boiling water until they are tender but still crisp, about 7 minutes. Drain well.

♦ Melt the butter in a medium-sized saucepan over a low heat. Add the spring onions and cook, stirring frequently, for 4 to 5 minutes, or until they are translucent. Remove the saucepan from the heat and stir in the paprika. Set aside.

♦ Combine the flour and soured cream in a small bowl until they are well mixed. Add the mixture to the spring onions. Add the salt. Simmer the mixture over a low heat for 5 minutes. Add the beans and simmer for 5 minutes longer. Serve hot.

Viennese Strudel

 גרמניה ואוסטריה

SERVES 8

The acknowledged champions of the baking world, the Viennese are proud of their strudel. Strudel dough should be so thin that newsprint can be read through it. Prepared strudel dough is now widely available.

2 prepared strudel sheets
225 g/8 oz melted butter
4 tbsp unflavoured dry breadcrumbs
4 cooking apples, peeled, cored and thinly sliced
150 g/5 oz sultanas
225 g/8 oz raspberries, fresh, frozen or tinned
225 g/8 oz chopped apricots, fresh or tinned
25 g/1 oz chopped unsalted roasted almonds
25 g/1 oz chopped walnuts
125 g/4 oz sugar
2 tsp cinnamon
2 tsp vanilla essence
15 g/$\frac{1}{2}$ oz icing sugar

Preheat the oven to 200°C/400°F/Gas 6. Spread one strudel sheet on a clean, lightly floured work surface. Brush the strudel sheet with half of the melted butter and sprinkle with 2 tablespoons of the breadcrumbs. Spread the second strudel sheet on top of the first. Brush the sheet with the remaining butter and sprinkle it with the remaining breadcrumbs.

♦ Combine the apples, sultanas, raspberries, apricots, almonds, walnuts, cinnamon and vanilla essence in a mixing bowl. (If tinned fruit is used, drain the syrup first.) Spread the mixture evenly over the surface of the top strudel sheet, leaving an inch border along each side. Roll up the strudel sheets like a Swiss roll.

♦ Place the strudel on a greased baking sheet. Bake at 200°C/400°F/Gas 6 for 30 minutes, then reduce the heat to 170°C/325°F/Gas 3 for another 35 minutes. Cool for 30 minutes before slicing. Sprinkle with icing sugar and serve.

German Austrian Festival Dinner

The menu below is one that might have been served in around 1900 in a Jewish home in Salzburg on a secular holiday such as New Year's Day or the Emperor's birthday. It could also have been served as a formal Sunday dinner. There is no starter or soup course because the dinner is very rich.

Wiener Schnitzel
Spaetzle with Roast Duck
Apple-Carrot Tzimmes
Hot Potato Salad
Brussels Sprouts Viennese
Fruit Salad

Wiener Schnitzel

SERVES 6

One of the most famous of Austrian dishes, Wiener Schnitzel is best made from veal escalopes or cutlets.

1.3 kg/3 lb very thin veal escalopes
350 ml/12 fl oz lemon juice
$\frac{1}{2}$ tsp salt
1 tsp black pepper
1 tbsp Worcestershire sauce
3 eggs, beaten
200 g/7 oz dry breadcrumbs
225 ml/8 fl oz vegetable oil

In a deep bowl, marinate the veal escalopes in the lemon juice for 1 hour.

♦ Drain the escalopes well and pat dry with kitchen paper. Sprinkle the escalopes with the salt, pepper and Worcestershire sauce. Dip the escalopes first in the beaten egg, then in the breadcrumbs, then in the egg again and finally in the breadcrumbs. The escalopes should be evenly coated.

♦ In a large, heavy frying pan, heat the oil over a medium heat. Add the escalopes and cook for 4 to 5 minutes on each side, or until they are crisp and golden brown. Serve garnished with lemon wedges.

Spaetzle with Roast Duck

SERVES 6

Spaetzle or spätzen are an extremely popular form of egg noodle. They go well with any sort of roast meat, but particularly with roast duck.

1-1.5 kg/2-3 lb duck, cut into two pieces, cleaned, with the fat retained
450 g/1 lb flour
2 tsp salt
5 eggs
450 ml/$\frac{3}{4}$ pt cold water
60 ml/2 fl oz lemon juice
125 ml/4 fl oz orange juice
3 tbsp currant or blackberry preserves
$\frac{1}{2}$ tsp black pepper

Preheat the oven to 170°C/325°F/Gas 3. Place the duck halves, skin-side up, in a roasting tin. Roast the duck for 1 hour.

♦ While the duck cooks, make the spaetzle. Place the flour in a large mixing bowl. Make a well in the centre of the mound. Sprinkle 1 teaspoon of the salt in the well. Break the eggs into the well and mix them into the flour. Gradually add the water (more or less as needed) and mix to form a stiff dough.

♦ Turn the dough out onto a lightly floured work surface and knead it vigorously until it is smooth and elastic. Roll or shape the dough into narrow strips. With a sharp knife, cut the strips into tiny pieces.

♦ Bring 3 L/5 pt water to a furious boil in a very large pot. Drop the spaetzle into the water. (Since each spaetzle must be able to float to the top of the water as it cooks, you may prefer to cook them in two or more pots of boiling water.) After the spaetzle rise to the top, boil for a further 15 minutes. Drain the spaetzle well and set them aside.

♦ After the duck has roasted for 1 hour, pour off the fat, reserving 125 ml/4 fl oz.

♦ In a small bowl, combine the lemon juice, orange juice, preserves and pepper. Brush the skin of the duck with the mixture. Return the duck halves to the oven, skin-side up, and roast for 1 hour longer, pouring off the fat from the pan twice during the cooking time.

♦ With a sharp knife, remove all the skin and meat from the duck halves and shred them coarsely. Discard the bones. Put the shredded meat and skin into a large serving bowl.

♦ Bring 3 L/5 pt of water to a furious boil in a large pot. Return the cooked spaetzle to the water for 1 minute. Drain the spaetzle well and add them to the shredded duck. Add the reserved duck fat and salt to taste. Toss well and serve hot.

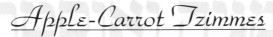

Apple-Carrot Tzimmes

SERVES 6

Tzimmes means mixture in Yiddish. The sweet and tangy flavour of the tzimmes is a good contrast to the richness of the Spaetzle with Roast Duck. Although served year round, this dish is traditional on Rosh Hashana. The sweetness symbolizes the hope for a sweet new year; the round carrot slices symbolize the hope for prosperity.

900 g/2 lb carrots, thinly sliced
2 dessert apples, peeled, cored and chopped
125 g/4 oz margarine
125 ml/4 fl oz water
80 g/3 oz seedless green grapes
3 tbsp honey
1 tbsp brown sugar
$\frac{1}{2}$ tsp cinnamon
$\frac{1}{4}$ tsp nutmeg

Combine all the ingredients in a small saucepan. Simmer over a very low heat for 90 minutes. Add more water as needed if the mixture starts to dry out. Serve hot.

Hot Potato Salad

SERVES 6 TO 8

This hearty potato salad will come as a delightful surprise to those who think that potato salad can only be served cold.

125 g/4 oz corned or salt beef, shredded
125 g/4 oz pastrami, shredded
125 ml/4 fl oz white wine vinegar
225 ml/8 fl oz water
2 tbsp sugar
2 tsp salt
1 tsp black pepper
900 g/2 lb cooked potatoes, peeled and cubed
6 tbsp chopped fresh parsley
1 tsp dried dill

Fry half the corned beef and pastrami in a large frying pan for 2 minutes. Add the vinegar, water, sugar, salt and pepper. Bring the liquid to a boil and cook, uncovered, for 10 minutes. Add the potatoes and cook for a further 8 minutes. Mix in the remaining corned beef and pastrami, and the parsley and dill. Serve hot.

Brussels Sprouts Viennese

SERVES 6

The unexpected addition of sweet red peppers gives this dish added zest. Use only fresh Brussels sprouts, and be careful not to overcook them.

450 g/1 lb fresh Brussels sprouts

1 sweet red pepper, seeded and cut into thin strips

50 g/2 oz margarine or butter

1 tsp sesame seeds

Cook the Brussels sprouts in a large saucepan of salted boiling water until they are tender but not mushy, about 5 to 8 minutes. Remove the Brussels sprouts from the water with a slotted spoon and drain well.

♦ Add the red pepper strips to the pan and cook until they are tender but still crisp, about 2 minutes. Drain well.

♦ Toss the Brussels sprouts and red pepper strips together in a serving bowl.

♦ Melt the margarine or butter in a small saucepan over a low heat. Add the sesame seeds and cook for 1 minute, stirring constantly. Pour the mixture over the Brussels sprouts and red pepper. Toss well. Serve hot.

Fruit Salad

SERVES 8

Apart from baked dishes, no dessert is so completely identified with the German-Austrian tradition as fruit salad.

225 g/8 oz dried pears

225 g/8 oz dried apricots

225 g/8 oz dried peaches

80 g/3 oz raisins

80 g/3 oz sultanas

200 g/7 oz dried prunes, stoned

450 g/1 lb sugar

1 cinnamon stick

rind of 1 lemon, cut into thin strips

Soak the dried fruits overnight in a large bowl with enough cold water to cover the fruit to the depth of at least 5cm/2 in.

♦ Pour the fruit soaking water into a large saucepan. Add the sugar, cinnamon and lemon rind. Bring the liquid to a boil over a medium heat, stirring until the sugar dissolves.

♦ Add the drained dried fruit and simmer for 10 minutes. Remove the fruit with a slotted spoon, and set aside. Boil the syrup mixture vigorously for 5 minutes. Remove the syrup from the heat and spoon it over the fruits immediately, while it is still hot. Chill thoroughly before serving.

German Austrian Sauerbraten Dinner

A traditional sauerbraten dinner is typical of German-Jewish fare from Vienna to Berlin. It is a hearty meal, ideal for staving off the cold in winter. To serve the sauerbraten on a Friday night, preparation should begin on the Monday before.

Lentil Soup
Beetroot with Horseradish
Sauerbraten
Sour Potatoes with Pickles
Berry Pudding

גרמניה ואוסטריה

Lentil Soup

SERVES 8

*Like their Gentile counterparts, the Jews of Germany and Austria have always been
fond of lentils and pulses in general. In a house of means, this hearty soup would
serve as a substantial first course. In a poorer household, it might be the entire meal,
served with boiled potatoes and black bread.*

675 g/1½ lb dried lentils

2.5 L/4¾ pt cold water

225 g/½ lb beef brisket, flank or neck

1 medium-sized leek, finely chopped

3 large carrots, finely chopped

1 parsnip, finely chopped

1 turnip, finely chopped

2 large celery stalks, finely chopped

4 tbsp beef dripping

175 g/6 oz finely chopped onion

2 tbsp flour

60 ml/2 fl oz white wine

4 all-beef kosher frankfurters, cut into pieces

1 tsp salt

1 tsp black pepper

Rinse and sort the lentils under cold water. In a large flameproof casserole, bring
the water to a boil. Add the lentils, beef, leek, carrots, parsnip, turnip and celery.
Return the mixture to the boil, reduce the heat, cover and simmer for 40 minutes.
♦ Melt the beef dripping in a large, heavy frying pan over a low heat. When it is very
hot, add the onions. Cook for 12 minutes, stirring frequently.
♦ Sprinkle the flour over the onions. Stir until the flour browns. Pour 225 ml/8 fl oz
of the lentil mixture over the onions and stir vigorously. Add the white wine and
cook 1 minute longer.
♦ Add the contents of the frying pan to the lentils. Simmer for 30 minutes.
♦ Add the frankfurters, salt and pepper to the soup. Simmer for a further 10
minutes. Serve hot with fresh crusty bread or melba toast.

Beetroot with Horseradish

SERVES 6

*The Germans and Austrians have probably found more uses for the humble red
beetroot than anyone else on Earth. This dish is traditionally served with Sauerbraten
or roasted game birds.*

450 g/1 lb boiled red beetroot, sliced

2 small apples, peeled, cored and diced

1 tsp caraway seeds

4 tsp drained, prepared white horseradish

½ tsp ground coriander

125 ml/4 fl oz red wine vinegar

2 tbsp sugar

1 tsp salt

In a large serving bowl combine the beetroot and apples. Add the caraway seeds, horseradish and coriander.

♦ In a large saucepan combine the vinegar, sugar and salt. Stir until the sugar has dissolved. Simmer over a very low heat for 8 minutes. Pour the liquid over the beetroot and apple mixture. Mix gently but thoroughly. Leave it to cool at room temperature for 30 minutes. Chill for 12 hours before serving.

Sauerbraten

SERVES 8—10

There are as many different versions of Sauerbraten as there are localities in Germany and Austria. You need to begin this dish 5 days before you want to serve it.

1.8 kg/4 lb beef brisket
450 ml/¾ pt red wine vinegar
450 ml/¾ pt white wine
2 tsp whole cloves
1 tsp whole black peppercorns
2 bay leaves
2 small onions, coarsely chopped
3 garlic cloves, quartered
1 large seedless orange with peel, sliced
60 ml/2 fl oz lemon juice
225 ml/8 fl oz water
1 tbsp salt
2 tbsp white cooking fat
225 g/8 oz whole cooked tomatoes
250 ml/8 fl oz tomato purée

Place the beef brisket in a large bowl or deep dish. Cover it with the vinegar, wine, cloves, peppercorns, bay leaves, onion, garlic, orange slices, lemon juice and water. Cover the bowl or dish tightly. Refrigerate for 4 days, turning the meat over daily.

♦ On the fifth day, remove the meat from the marinade and pat dry with kitchen towels. Reserve the marinade. Melt the white cooking fat in a large flameproof casserole or heavy pan. Add the meat and brown well on all sides. Add the tomatoes, tomato purée and reserved marinade. Cover tightly and simmer for 2½ hours, or until the meat is tender.

♦ Remove the meat from the casserole or pan and leave it to stand for ten minutes before slicing.

♦ Pass 750 ml/1¼ pt of the cooking liquid through a sieve into a saucepan. Discard any solids remaining in the sieve. Bring the liquid to a boil and simmer for 5 minutes. Serve this as gravy with the sliced sauerbraten.

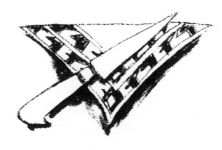

Sour Potatoes with Pickles

SERVES 6—8

All the vegetables in a traditional Sauerbraten should take on, to a greater or lesser degree, the tangy flavour of the main course. This uniquely Austrian recipe for potatoes should be made on the day the meal is served. The sourer the pickles, the better the dish.

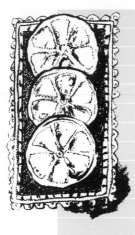

6 large potatoes

2 tbsp lemon juice

125 g/4 oz steak

450 ml/$\frac{3}{4}$ pt beef stock

70 g/$2\frac{1}{2}$ oz Spanish or red onion, diced

2 tbsp flour

$\frac{1}{4}$ tsp dried marjoram

$\frac{1}{2}$ tsp salt

$\frac{1}{2}$ tsp black pepper

$\frac{1}{2}$ tsp dried parsley

$\frac{1}{4}$ tsp dried thyme

1 large bay leaf

3 sour pickled cucumbers, finely chopped

Scrub the potatoes and cook them in a large pot of boiling water for 15 minutes, or until the potatoes are tender but not mushy. Drain well. Cut the potatoes into medium-sized chunks and put them into a serving bowl. Sprinkle the potatoes with the lemon juice and set aside.

♦ In a medium-sized heavy frying pan, brown the steak in 125 ml/4 fl oz of the beef stock for about 2 minutes. Add the onions and flour and brown over a low heat for 10 minutes. Turn off the heat.

♦ Remove the steak and cut it into small pieces. Return the steak pieces to the frying pan. Add the remaining beef broth and the marjoram, salt, pepper, parsley, thyme, bay leaf and pickles. Stir well. Cover the frying pan and simmer for 30 minutes.

♦ Pour the mixture over the potatoes. Toss well and serve.

Berry Pudding

SERVES 8

This deliciously light dessert is a good way to end a heavy meal. The fruit can be varied with the season.

675 g/$1\frac{1}{2}$ lb fresh or frozen raspberries

675 g/$1\frac{1}{2}$ lb fresh or frozen strawberries

450 g/1 lb fresh or tinned peaches, finely chopped

60 ml/2 fl oz Triple Sec or other orange-flavoured liqueur

2 egg whites

If you are using frozen berries, thaw them first and drain well. If you are using fresh peaches, peel them and remove the stones. If you are using tinned peaches, drain well. Purée the raspberries and strawberries in a liquidizer or food processor.

♦ Beat the egg whites in a mixing bowl until they are stiff. Add the liqueur. Beat for a further 30 seconds. Add the berry purée to the egg white mixture. Mix gently until the purée is evenly distributed.

♦ Half fill 8 dessert glasses with the berry mixture. Spoon in a layer of diced peaches. Top with more berry mixture. Chill for 1 hour before serving.

German Austrian Dairy Lunch

The German and Austrian Jews showed a particular affinity in their cuisine for nearly all varieties of permitted fish. The menu below makes use of both pike and herring, and features the unusual accompaniment of red cabbage with apples. The chocolate pear dessert is a speciality of Berlin.

German Herring Salad
Baked Stuffed Pike
Red Cabbage with Apples
Green Bean Salad
Chocolate Pears

German Herring Salad

SERVES 6

This piquant herring salad is a delicious way to start a dairy meal. Serve it on a bed of lettuce with thin rounds of crusty bread.

400-450 g/14-16 oz herring fillets

70 g/2½ oz cooked beetroot, diced

3 spring onions (including tops), diced

2 tbsp white wine vinegar

½ tsp dried tarragon

½ tsp dried dill

2 tbsp olive oil

60 ml/2 fl oz lemon juice

½ tsp black pepper

60 ml/2 fl oz orange juice

1 tbsp Dijon-style mustard

Combine all the ingredients in a liquidizer or food processor and chop finely. Spoon the salad into a serving bowl, cover tightly and refrigerate for at least 1 hour before serving.

Baked Stuffed Pike

SERVES 6

Pike is one of the finest of freshwater fish. This recipe, which originated in the Baden area of Germany, is a favourite among German Jews.

175 g/6 oz finely chopped onions

6 tbsp melted butter

3 fresh garlic cloves, diced

125 g/4 oz finely chopped mushrooms

40 g/1½ oz seasoned soft breadcrumbs

60 ml/2 fl oz milk

6 anchovies, ground to a paste

1 tbsp capers

2 tbsp finely chopped parsley

25 g/1 oz grated Parmesan cheese

1.8 kg/4 lb yellow pike, cleaned and scaled, without backbone, but with head and tail left intact

150 ml/¼ pt soured cream

1 tsp salt

1 tsp black pepper

3 tbsp lemon juice

Prepare the stuffing first. In a medium-sized frying pan, brown the onions in the butter. Cook for 2 to 3 minutes. Stir in the mushrooms and cook for a further 5 minutes.

♦ In a large mixing bowl, combine the breadcrumbs, milk, anchovies, capers, parsley and Parmesan cheese. Mix thoroughly. Set the stuffing aside.

♦ Preheat the oven to 220°C/425°F/Gas 7. Rinse the fish inside and out, and pat completely dry. Fill the cavity of the fish with the stuffing. Pour the butter, mushrooms and onions over the fish. Bake the fish for 45 to 50 minutes, basting with the pan juices every 5 to 7 minutes.

♦ While the fish is cooking, combine the soured cream, salt, pepper and lemon juice in a small bowl. Chill.

♦ Remove the fish from the oven. Remove the stuffing from the cavity of the fish and place it in a large mixing bowl. Add half the fish fat and half the onions and mushrooms from the baking tin. Mix well. Put the stuffing back into the fish. Reduce the oven temperature to 130°C/250°F/Gas ½. Return the fish to the oven for 5 minutes.

♦ Pour the remaining fish fat, along with the remaining mushrooms and onions from the baking tin into a small saucepan. Add the chilled soured cream, mix and cook over a low heat, stirring frequently until heated through. Do not allow the sauce to boil.

♦ Arrange the fish on a serving plate. Pour some of the sauce over the fish. Serve the remainder of the fish sauce separately.

Red Cabbage with Apples

SERVES 6

Red cabbage is a staple of the German-Austrian Jewish diet, much as potatoes are for the Irish. There are an infinite number of ways to prepare it. This recipe is traditionally served with dairy lunches. It is also often served at Chanuka.

1 large red cabbage, shredded
2 tbsp sugar
1 tsp salt
50 g/2 oz butter
125 ml/4 fl oz raspberry vinegar
3 large cooking apples, peeled, cored and diced
4 tbsp chopped spring onions
1 bay leaf
1 whole clove
1.5 L/2½ pt boiling water
4 tbsp blackberry preserves
60 ml/2 fl oz dry red wine

In a large bowl, combine the shredded cabbage with the sugar, salt and vinegar. Toss until the cabbage is evenly coated with the vinegar mixture.

♦ In a large flameproof casserole, melt the butter. Add the apples and spring onions and cook over a very low heat for 8 minutes, stirring frequently. Add the cabbage and vinegar mixture, the bay leaf and the clove. Stir in the boiling water. Cover and simmer over a low heat for 90 minutes.

♦ Add the blackberry preserves and red wine. Simmer for a further 30 minutes. Serve in a large glass or porcelain bowl.

Green Bean Salad

SERVES 6

This light salad is the perfect accompaniment to a hearty German-style dairy meal. It is particularly nice on hot summer days.

675 g/1½ lb fresh green beans, trimmed and halved

For the dressing:

4 tbsp olive oil

2 tbsp white wine vinegar

60 ml/2 fl oz vegetable stock or water

½ tsp salt

1 tsp cayenne pepper

1 tbsp finely chopped fresh dill or 1 tsp dried dill

2 tsp chopped fresh parsley

1 tbsp Dijon-style mustard

Cook the green beans in a large pot of boiling water until they are tender but still crisp. Drain well. Put the green beans into a large serving bowl.
◆ In a mixing bowl combine the olive oil, vinegar, stock or water, salt, cayenne pepper, dill, parsley and mustard. Mix well.
◆ Pour the dressing over the green beans and toss well. Chill for 1 hour before serving.

Chocolate Pears

SERVES 6

This unique dessert originated in Bavaria, near the Austrian border. It should be served immediately.

For the chocolate sauce:

125 g/4 oz plain chocolate

8 tbsp golden syrup

25 g/1 oz margarine

For the dessert:

900 g/2 lb tinned pear halves, drained

950 ml/32 fl oz whipping cream

125 g/4 oz sugar

450 ml/¾ pt vanilla ice-cream

First make the chocolate sauce. Place the plain chocolate, golden syrup and margarine in a bowl over a saucepan of hot water. As the chocolate and syrup melt, beat the mixture until it is smooth.
◆ Line the bottom of a large glass bowl with the pears. Pour 125 ml/4 fl oz of the chocolate sauce over the pears.
◆ Whip the cream and sugar together until the mixture is soft and velvety. Spoon half the whipped cream over the pears.
◆ Spoon small pieces of the ice-cream over the whipped cream. Top with the remaining whipped cream. Drizzle the remaining chocolate sauce over the dessert and serve immediately. Garnish with sponge fingers or sweet tea biscuits.

Wiener Schnitzel ABOVE *is one of the most famous
of Austrian dishes (page 134).*

♦

Brussels Sprouts Viennese BELOW *is a colourful
and tasty vegetable dish (page 136).*

*Apple-Carrot Tzimmes has a sweet and sour
flavour that provides an excellent contrast to the
richness of Spaetzle with Roast Duck at a German
Austrian Festival Dinner (page 135).*

Lentil Soup ABOVE LEFT *makes a substantial first
course at a Sauerbraten Dinner (page 138).*

♦

Sour Potatoes with Pickles ABOVE RIGHT *provides a
tangy accompaniment to Sauerbraten (page 140).*

♦

Chocolate Pears BELOW *is a unique dessert
originating in Bavaria (page 144).*

France
and Italy

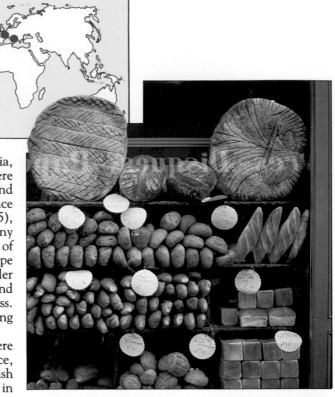

FRANCE   The Jewish communities of Marseilles, Aix, Arles, Avignon, Nîmes, Narbonne and other cities in Provence flourished from 800 on. They were principally trading communities, doing business with Egypt, Syria, India, China and Persia. Other Jewish communities were founded in Paris, Troyes, Nice, Bordeaux, Bayonne and Lyons. From the tenth to the thirteenth centuries, France was a major centre of Jewish learning. Rashi (1040-1105), the greatest of Talmudic scholars, lived in Troyes. Many Jews emigrated to the Alsace region and the cities of Strasbourg, Metz, Verdun and Nancy to escape persecution in Germany from 1100 to 1500. Under Napoleon, French Jews were granted full citizenship, and many rose to prominence in government and business. Many Jews emigrated to France from North Africa, during the period of French control there.

During World War II some 100,000 French Jews were exterminated. The population has grown rapidly since, however, and today 700,000 Jews, half the Jewish population in Europe, live in France. Nearly half live in Paris, with the rest chiefly in Marseilles, Lyons, Nice, Toulon and Strasbourg. There are more than two hundred synagogues in France and more than fifty kosher restaurants. The Jewish area of the Marais district of Paris is called the Pletzel, and Jews have lived there since the eleventh century.

French-Jewish cooking is an interesting blend of Eastern European and Continental cuisine. The more assimilated Jews frequently ignored the kosher laws, but other simply modified standard French dishes to meet their dietary requirements. A kosher version of bouillabaisse is included here, a dish that is traditionally made with shellfish.

ITALY   The word ghetto is derived from the Italian, where it first referred to the Jewish quarter of Venice. In fact, Jews have lived in Italy since Roman times. They developed highly successful communities renowned for their scholarship, and the first Hebrew book was printed in Italy in 1475. Jews in Italy traditionally enjoyed a great deal of liberty and freedom from persecution, although many were killed during World War II.

Italian Jewish cooking is a distinct branch of Italian cooking, just as, say, Sicilian cooking is. There are Jewish restaurants in Milan and Rome. Fried Artichokes Jewish-Style are as synonymous with Jewish cuisine in Italy as Chopped Liver is in the English-speaking world.

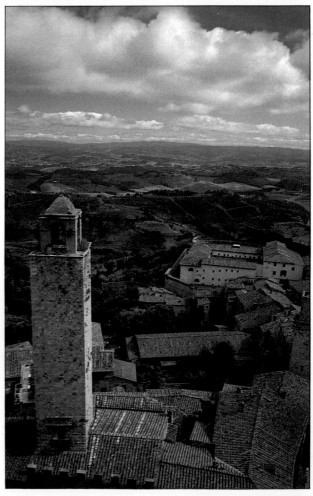

The Jews who settled in France and Italy adapted many of the classic dishes they found there to kosher requirements.

Baby Lamb ABOVE *is traditionally served at an Italian Passover Dinner (page 164).*

◆

Jewish Artichokes BELOW *is one of the most famous of Italian Jewish dishes (page 165).*

French Jewish Supper

Many French Jews contend that Jewish chefs had a profound influence on the style of classic French cuisine that reached its peak in the late nineteenth century. Below is a menu reminiscent of that period. It contains the famous Pâté Rothschild.

Pâté Rothschild
Vegetable Garlic Basil Soup
Braised Veal Chops
Braised Peas with Onions and Lettuce
Stuffed Mushrooms Provençal
Soufflé Grand Marnier

Pâté Rothschild

SERVES 6—8

The House of Rothschild, world-famous for its financiers and philanthropists, began in Frankfurt in the sixteenth century. The family home was in the Judengasse (Jew Street), identified by a red shield, from which the family took its name. The five sons of Mayer Amschel Rothschild established branches of the family business in Germany, Austria, England, Italy and France. They were as well-known for their philanthropic work for Jewish causes as they were for their fabulous wealth.

450 g/1 lb fresh chicken livers, finely chopped

450 g/1 lb fresh calf's liver, finely chopped

2 eggs, beaten

100 g/3½ oz cooked haricot beans, puréed

2 tbsp lemon juice

4 tbsp non-dairy cream substitute

1 garlic clove, finely chopped

1 bay leaf, crumbled

¼ tsp salt

¼ tsp black pepper

125 ml/4 fl oz melted chicken fat

60 ml/2 fl oz brandy

60 ml/2 fl oz dark sherry

Preheat the oven to 170°C/325°F/Gas 3. Combine all the ingredients in a large wooden mixing bowl and mix thoroughly.

♦ Pack the pâté mixture into a small loaf tin. Smooth the top. Bake for 1½ hours.

♦ Remove the pâté from the oven and leave it to cool. Invert the loaf tin and turn out the pâté. Cover and chill for at least 3 hours before serving.

Vegetable Garlic Basil Soup

SERVES 8

This hearty traditional French soup can be a meal in itself. Serve with crusty bread.

5 tbsp olive oil

175 g/6 oz finely chopped onions

5 garlic cloves, finely chopped

2.35 L/4 pt water

100 g/3½ oz cooked haricot beans

450 g/1 lb fresh tomatoes, peeled, seeded and coarsely chopped

175 g/6 oz coarsely chopped carrots

125 g/4 oz diced new potatoes

4 tbsp finely chopped spring onions

50 g/2 oz coarsely chopped celery, including leaves

150 g/5 oz trimmed fresh green beans, quartered

175 g/6 oz thinly sliced courgettes

4 tbsp dried basil

2 tbsp tomato purée

½ tsp salt

½ tsp black pepper

Heat 2 tablespoons olive oil in a large saucepan. Add the onions and garlic and fry over a low heat for 5 minutes. Add the remaining ingredients, including the remaining olive oil, and simmer over a medium heat for 30 minutes, stirring occasionally. Serve hot.

Braised Veal Chops with Parsley Dressing

SERVES 6—8

These braised veal chops exemplify the subtle flavours of French Jewish cuisine.

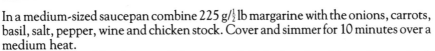

250 g/9 oz margarine
175 g/6 oz finely chopped onions
80 g/3 oz finely chopped carrots
1 tsp dried basil
$\frac{1}{2}$ tsp salt
$\frac{1}{2}$ tsp black pepper
350 ml/12 fl oz white wine
225 ml/8 oz chicken stock
4 tbsp vegetable oil
40 g/$1\frac{1}{2}$ oz unflavoured soft breadcrumbs
70 g/$2\frac{1}{2}$ oz minced salt beef
1 tsp lemon juice
3 tbsp finely chopped parsley
8 loin veal chops, 2.5 cm/1 in thick

In a medium-sized saucepan combine 225 g/$\frac{1}{2}$ lb margarine with the onions, carrots, basil, salt, pepper, wine and chicken stock. Cover and simmer for 10 minutes over a medium heat.
♦ Heat the vegetable oil in a small frying pan. Add the breadcrumbs and brown for 3 to 5 minutes over a low heat. Stir in the salt beef, lemon juice, parsley and the remaining 25 g/1 oz margarine. Cook over a low heat, stirring frequently, for 2 to 3 minutes.
♦ In a large flameproof casserole, arrange the veal chops in a single layer. Pour the stock mixture over the chops, and then the seasoned breadcrumb mixture.
♦ Cover and cook over a medium heat for 40 minutes, or until the veal is tender.

Braised Peas with Onions and Lettuce

SERVES 6—8

This simple dish should be made with fresh peas, not frozen or tinned.

1 small head soft lettuce, coarsely torn
450 g/1 lb fresh peas
225 g/$\frac{1}{2}$ lb small onions
4 tbsp coarsely chopped parsley
80 g/3 oz margarine
125 ml/4 oz water
$\frac{1}{2}$ tsp salt
$\frac{1}{2}$ tsp sugar
1 tbsp olive oil

Combine all the ingredients in a medium-sized saucepan and toss to distribute evenly. Cover and simmer over a low heat for 5 minutes.
♦ Remove the lid and toss again. Simmer for a further 3 to 5 minutes and serve.

155

Stuffed Mushrooms Provençal

SERVES 6—8

An excellent side dish, these mushrooms can also be served as a first course.

45 to 50 large mushrooms, stems removed and set aside
4 tbsp finely chopped spring onions
4 tbsp finely chopped shallots
225 g/8 oz finely chopped fresh spinach
2 tbsp chopped parsley
50 g/2 oz margarine
2 tbsp flour
60 ml/2 fl oz white wine
3 tbsp olive oil

Preheat the oven to 180°C/350°F/Gas 4. Finely chop the mushroom stems. In a small saucepan, combine the spring onions, shallots, spinach, parsley, margarine, flour, white wine and olive oil. Mix thoroughly and cook over a low heat until the margarine melts. Cover and simmer for 2 minutes.

♦ Add the mushroom stems. Mix thoroughly and cover. Simmer the filling over a low heat for a further 5 minutes.

♦ Place approximately 1 teaspoon of the filling in each mushroom cap. Place the filled caps on greased baking sheets and bake for 15 minutes. Serve hot.

Soufflé Grand Marnier

SERVES 6—8

The use of margarine instead of butter makes the soufflé pareve; butter could be used if the soufflé is to be served with a dairy meal.

10 egg yolks
225 g/8 oz sugar
125 ml/4 fl oz Grand Marnier liqueur
$1\frac{1}{2}$ tbsp grated orange rind
14 egg whites
$\frac{1}{2}$ tsp cream of tartar
50 g/2 oz softened margarine
$1\frac{1}{2}$ tbsp castor sugar

Beat the egg yolks in the top of a double boiler. Gradually beat in 4 tablespoons of the sugar until the mixture is a light lemon colour.

♦ Fill the lower compartment of the double boiler halfway with water. Bring the water to a simmer and cook the egg yolk mixture over it, stirring gently until the mixture thickens and becomes very hot.

♦ Stir the liqueur and the orange rind into the egg yolk mixture. Pour the mixture into a medium-sized metal mixing bowl and chill in the freezer until very cold.

♦ Beat the egg whites and cream of tartar together in a large mixing bowl until they are stiff. Gently fold the egg yolk mixture into the egg whites.

♦ Preheat the oven to 220°C/425°F/Gas 7. Thoroughly grease a 2.85 L/2¾ pt soufflé dish with the softened margarine. Evenly sprinkle the sides and bottom of the dish with the remaining sugar. Spoon the soufflé mixture into the dish. Bake in the centre of the oven for 3 minutes. Reduce the heat to 200°C/400°F/Gas 6 and bake for a further 30 minutes, or until puffed and lightly browned. Sprinkle with the castor sugar and serve immediately.

French
Jewish Dairy Supper

This dairy meal includes kosher versions of two standards of French cuisine: Onion Soup and Fisherman's Stew, an adaptation of the famed Bouillabaisse.

Chopped Herring Marseilles
French Onion Soup
Fisherman's Stew with Rouille
Asparagus with Hollandaise Sauce
Raspberry Mousse
Chocolate Mousse

Chopped Herring Marseilles

SERVES 6—8

This French version of herring salad is a perfect first course for a dairy meal.

8 large salt herring fillets
70 g/2½ oz finely chopped onion
2 apples, peeled, cored and finely chopped
3 hard-boiled eggs, finely chopped
4 tbsp vinegar
3 slices white bread, trimmed and shredded
2 tsp sugar
2½ tbsp olive oil

Soak the herring overnight in cold water in a large mixing bowl. Drain well and chop finely.

♦ In a mixing bowl combine the herring with the remaining ingredients. Mix thoroughly until the consistency is even throughout. Cover and chill for at least 4 hours before serving.

French Onion Soup

SERVES 8

Served in individual bowls topped with melted cheese, this soup is a French classic.

2 tbsp vegetable oil
50 g/2 oz butter
900 g/2 lb onions, coarsely chopped
2 tbsp flour
1.9 L/3¼ pt vegetable stock
½ tsp salt
12 slices Emmental cheese
16 thin slices cut from a French stick loaf
2 tsp olive oil
2 garlic cloves, finely chopped

Heat the vegetable oil and butter in a large deep saucepan. Add the onions and fry over a medium heat for 5 minutes. Reduce the heat to low and simmer for a further 20 minutes, stirring frequently.

♦ Sprinkle the onions with the flour and continue cooking, stirring constantly, for 3 minutes.

♦ Add the vegetable stock and salt. Simmer, covered, for 35 minutes over a low heat.

♦ While the soup simmers, coarsely chop 4 of the cheese slices. Preheat the oven to 170°C/325°F/Gas 3.

♦ Brush the bread slices with the olive oil and arrange them in a single layer on a baking sheet. Sprinkle the bread with the garlic and the chopped cheese. Bake for 15 minutes and set aside.

♦ When the soup is done, place 2 bread slices in each of 8 individual deep ovenproof soup bowls or ramekins. Fill each bowl with soup and top with a slice of cheese. Place the bowls on the centre rack of the oven and raise the heat to 180°C/350°F/Gas 4. Bake for 5 to 7 minutes or until the cheese begins to soften and turn brown. Remove the bowls from the oven, allow to cool for 1 minute and serve.

Fisherman's Stew with Rouille

SERVES 8

Bouillabaisse, the famous French fish stew, is made with both fish and shellfish. This kosher adaptation is made with fish alone. Like Bouillabaisse, it is served with rouille, a piquant condiment mixture that is added to each serving to taste.

900 g/2 lb fresh halibut steaks

900 g/2 lb red snapper, cleaned

900 g/2 lb sea bass, cleaned

900 g/2 lb haddock steaks

900 g/2 lb cod steaks

900 g/2 lb pike steaks

900 g/2 lb trout, cleaned

9 tbsp olive oil

275 g/10 oz onions, coarsely chopped

125 g/4 oz thinly sliced leeks

6 garlic cloves, finely chopped

1.6 L/55 fl oz water

450 ml/$\frac{3}{4}$ pt white wine

1.4 kg/3 lb tomatoes, peeled, seeded and coarsely chopped

1 tsp grated orange rind

1 tsp dried thyme

1 tbsp roughly chopped parsley

1 bay leaf

$\frac{1}{4}$ tsp saffron threads

$\frac{1}{2}$ tsp salt

$\frac{1}{2}$ tsp black pepper

2 green peppers, coarsely chopped

$\frac{1}{2}$ tsp Tabasco sauce

8 tbsp chopped pimento

3 tbsp unflavoured breadcrumbs

400 g/14 oz cooked rice

Trim the skin and bones from the fish steaks. Fillet the whole fish. Cut the fish steaks and fillets into 2.5 cm/1 in cubes. Reserve the trimmings, heads and bones.
♦ Heat 3 tablespoons of the olive oil in a large, 5.3 L/9 pt saucepan. Add the onions, leeks and 2 chopped garlic cloves. Cook over a low heat, stirring occasionally, for 5 minutes.
♦ Add 1.4 L/48 fl oz of the water and the white wine and reserved fish trimmings to the pan. Cover and simmer over a low heat for 5 minutes.
♦ Add the tomatoes, orange rind, thyme, parsley, bay leaf, saffron, salt and pepper. Raise the heat slightly and simmer, covered, for 15 minutes. Remove the lid and simmer for a further 10 minutes.
♦ Prepare the rouille. Combine the remaining garlic with the green peppers, Tabasco sauce, pimentos, remaining olive oil and breadcrumbs. Mix well.
♦ Put the rouille mixture into a saucepan and add 200 ml/7 fl oz water. Simmer over a moderate heat for 10 minutes. Put the rouille into a serving bowl and set aside.
♦ When the fish stock is ready, pour it through a muslin-lined sieve into another saucepan. Discard the solids remaining in the muslin.
♦ Bring the strained stock to a boil over a medium heat. Add the fish pieces and cook for 10 minutes. Reduce the heat to low and cook for a further 5 minutes.
♦ Put some of the cooked rice into each individual soup bowl. Ladle the soup on top. Serve with rouille.

Asparagus with Hollandaise Sauce

SERVES 8

When making Hollandaise sauce, never let the sauce boil, or it will curdle. Use the thinnest, freshest asparagus you can find.

900 g/2 lb thin green asparagus
175 g/6 oz butter
3 egg yolks
1 tbsp lemon juice
1 tbsp double cream
$\frac{1}{4}$ tsp salt
$\frac{1}{4}$ tsp ground white pepper

Fill a medium-sized saucepan to a depth of 8 cm/3 in with water.
♦ Add the asparagus, cover and simmer over a medium heat for 12 minutes.
♦ Meanwhile, melt the butter in a small saucepan and set aside, keeping the butter warm over a very low heat.
♦ In a small mixing bowl, beat the egg yolks and lemon juice together for 3 to 5 minutes, or until the mixture thickens.
♦ Beat the egg yolk mixture into the melted butter over a very low heat. Beat in the cream, salt and white pepper. Remove from the heat and let the sauce thicken for 5 minutes, stirring gently but frequently.
♦ Drain the cooked asparagus well and place in a large deep serving dish. Top with the Hollandaise sauce. Serve warm.

Raspberry Mousse

SERVES 6—8

Frozen raspberries can be used in this adaptation of the traditional French recipe.

350 g/$\frac{3}{4}$ lb fresh raspberries
4 egg yolks, beaten
125 ml/4 fl oz water
1 tsp arrowroot
175 g/6 oz sugar
60 ml/2 fl oz framboise or blackberry liqueur
450 ml/$\frac{3}{4}$ pt double cream
1 tbsp vegetable oil

Crush the raspberries and push them through a fine sieve into a bowl. Discard any solids that remain in the sieve.
♦ In a small saucepan, combine the beaten egg yolks with the water and arrowroot. Stir briskly over a medium heat and gradually add the sugar, stirring until it is completely dissolved. Add the crushed raspberries and the liqueur. Stir well, cover and cook over a low heat for 5 minutes.
♦ In a large mixing bowl, whip the cream until it is stiff.
♦ Gradually spoon the heated raspberry mixture into the cream, stirring constantly until they are thoroughly combined.
♦ With the vegetable oil grease a large pudding mould. Pour the raspberry mousse into the mould. Freeze the mousse until it is solid. Remove from the freezer and leave it to thaw for 1 hour before serving.

Chocolate Mousse

SERVES 8

One of the most famous of French desserts, Chocolate Mousse takes quite a long time to make.

8 egg yolks
175 g/6 oz castor sugar
1½ tbsp brandy
1½ tbsp Triple Sec liqueur
350 g/12 oz plain chocolate, chopped
3½ tbsp strong coffee
225 g/½ lb unsalted butter, softened
8 egg whites
350 ml/12 fl oz double cream

In a large flameproof mixing bowl, beat the egg yolks, 125 g/4 oz sugar, brandy and Triple Sec into a pale frothy mixture.

♦ Set the bowl over a saucepan of simmering water and continue beating for 6 minutes, or until the mixture is hot.

♦ Place the bowl inside a larger bowl filled with crushed ice and beat for 5 minutes, or until the mixture has a thick creamy consistency. Set aside.

♦ Melt the chocolate pieces with the coffee in a small saucepan over a low heat. When the chocolate has completely melted, beat in the softened butter until the mixture thickens and is smooth and even.

♦ Spoon the chocolate mixture into the egg yolk mixture and beat gently until creamy.

♦ In another bowl, beat the egg whites until they are stiff. Gradually fold them into the chocolate mixture. Cover the bowl and chill.

♦ In a medium-sized metal mixing bowl, whip the cream together with the remaining sugar until it has a soft but fairly firm consistency.

♦ Spoon the chocolate mousse into tulip or dessert glasses and top with the whipped cream. Chill before serving.

Italian Passover Dinner

The Italian Jews have developed a cuisine that is as distinct from the rest of Italian cooking as 'Jewish food' is in Britain and the United States. In fact, in the large Italian cities there are restaurants serving Jewish specialities just as there are Jewish delicatessens in other countries. Italian Jewish food is quite different from what even a French Jew would consider Jewish cooking.

Passover Chicken Soup
Sea Bass in Jelly
Sautéed Spinach
Baby Lamb
Jewish Artichokes
Matzoh Omelette

Passover Chicken Soup

SERVES 8

This delicious soup is the traditional first course at a Passover meal in Italy.

1 chicken breast, skinned and boned, and finely chopped
1 egg, beaten
4 tbsp matzoh meal
3 tbsp water
$\frac{1}{4}$ tsp salt
$\frac{1}{4}$ tsp grated nutmeg
$\frac{1}{4}$ tsp ground cinnamon
2.3 L/4 pt chicken stock
125 g/4 oz rice
8 hard-boiled egg yolks

In a large mixing bowl, combine the chopped chicken meat with the egg, matzoh meal, water, salt, nutmeg and cinnamon. Mix well. Cover the mixing bowl and chill for 30 minutes.
♦ Shape the chicken mixture into small balls approximately 2 cm/$\frac{3}{4}$ in in diameter. In a large saucepan, bring the stock to a boil over a high heat. Add the rice and chicken balls. Reduce the heat to medium and cover. Simmer for 20 minutes.
♦ Place one hard-boiled egg yolk in the centre of each of eight deep soup bowls. Ladle the soup over the top. Serve hot.

Sea Bass in Jelly

SERVES 6—8

This Italian speciality is similar to the more familiar gefilte fish.

2.3-2.7 kg/5-6 lb sea bass
175 g/6 oz diced onion
150 g/5 oz diced celery
80 g/3 oz sliced carrots
1 tbsp lemon juice
$\frac{1}{2}$ tsp ground white pepper
$\frac{1}{2}$ tsp salt
700 ml/24 fl oz cold water

Clean and fillet the fish. Reserve the head and bones. In a medium-sized saucepan, place the fish fillets, reserved head and bones, onion, celery, carrots, lemon juice, pepper, salt and water. Simmer over a low heat for 20 minutes.
♦ Carefully remove the pieces of fish fillet with a slotted spoon and place them in a deep medium-sized glass or ceramic, but not metal, dish. Cover and chill.
♦ Strain the stock through a fine sieve. Discard the solids remaining in the sieve. Return the stock to the pan and bring to a boil over a high heat. Cook for 15 to 20 minutes, or until the liquid is reduced by about half.
♦ Pour the stock over the fish pieces and chill for two hours or more. The stock will gel as it chills. Serve cold with mayonnaise and/or lemon wedges.

Sautéed Spinach

SERVES 6—8

It is customary in Italy to serve a green vegetable dish halfway through dinner. This spinach dish is traditional at Passover.

1.4 kg/3 lb fresh spinach
3 garlic cloves, quartered
125 ml/4 fl oz olive oil
$\frac{1}{4}$ tsp salt
$\frac{1}{4}$ tsp black pepper

Remove any tough stems and blemished leaves from the spinach. Rinse the spinach thoroughly to remove all grit. Drain well.

♦ In a large, heavy frying pan, brown the garlic in the olive oil over a low heat. Add the spinach leaves, salt and pepper. Cook for 10 minutes, stirring frequently. Serve immediately.

Baby Lamb

SERVES 8

This dish is traditionally made with chops from a young goat, an animal that is kosher. But the recipe is often adapted to lamb, which is more easily available.

1.8 kg/4 lb lamb rib chops
3 tbsp olive oil
$\frac{1}{2}$ tsp salt
$\frac{1}{4}$ tsp black pepper
3 tbsp coarsely chopped parsley
2 garlic cloves, finely chopped
350 ml/12 fl oz cold water
2 egg yolks
2 tbsp lemon juice

Place the lamb chops in a large heavy frying pan. Add the oil, salt, pepper, parsley and garlic. Pour the water over the meat and spices, cover, and simmer over a low heat for 1 hour.

♦ In a small mixing bowl, combine the egg yolks and lemon juice. Pour over the lamb and cover. Simmer for another 3 minutes and serve.

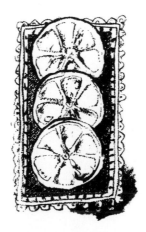

Jewish Artichokes

SERVES 6—8

This artichoke dish is as closely identified with Jewish cooking in Italy as Chopped Liver is with Jewish cooking in the English-speaking world.

12 fresh artichokes, trimmed
1 tbsp salt
1 tbsp black pepper
700 ml/24 fl oz olive oil
3 tbsp lemon juice
125 ml/4 fl oz water

Sprinkle the artichokes with the salt and pepper, making sure that some of the seasoning finds its way between the individual leaves.

♦ Put the oil in a medium-sized saucepan. Place over a medium heat. Put as many artichokes in the pan, stem down, as will fit comfortably. Cook for 25 minutes. As the artichokes cook, sprinkle them periodically with the lemon juice and water until these are used up.

♦ After 25 minutes, carefully invert the artichokes, two at a time, in the oil. Remove when the leaves open and turn golden brown.

Matzoh Omelette

SERVES 8

This delicious omelette can be served as the dessert course at a Passover dinner, or on its own as a lunch or breakfast.

8 plain matzohs
12 eggs, beaten
$\frac{1}{2}$ tsp salt
3 tbsp pine kernels
70 g/$2\frac{1}{2}$ oz sultanas
finely grated rind of 1 lemon
2 tbsp vegetable oil
125 g/4 oz sugar
$1\frac{1}{2}$ tsp ground cinnamon

Soak the matzohs in water for 3 to 5 minutes or until soft. Drain well.

♦ In a large mixing bowl, combine the softened matzohs, eggs, salt, pine kernels, sultanas and lemon rind. Mix well.

♦ Heat the vegetable oil in a large heavy frying pan over a low heat.

♦ Pour the omelette mixture into the frying pan and cover. Cook for 8 minutes or until the omelette is solid. Sprinkle with the sugar and cinnamon. Fold the omelette in half and remove from the pan. Serve warm.

Italian Chanuka Dinner

It is traditional in Italy for a Chanuka menu to include a variety of fried foods in commemoration of the sanctified oil that miraculously burned for eight days when the Temple in Jerusalem was rededicated in 165 BCE, after the Maccabees defeated the Syrians.

Crêpes with Tuna

Holiday Fried Chicken

Rice with Raisins

Chanuka Fritters

Crêpes with Tuna

SERVES 6—8

This unusual recipe is a Chanuka favourite with the Italian Jews. Use imported Italian tuna packed in oil for the best results.

2 × 200 g/6½ oz tins Italian tuna, drained

50 g/2 oz tin anchovies, drained

2 tbsp chopped parsley

½ tsp salt

½ tsp pepper

6 eggs, beaten

125 g/4 oz flour

225 ml/8 fl oz cold water

2 tsp finely chopped onion

2 tbsp vegetable oil

In a medium-sized mixing bowl, combine the tuna, anchovies, parsley, salt and pepper. Flake with a fork and mix until evenly blended. Set the filling aside.
♦ In another mixing bowl, combine the eggs, flour, water and onions. Mix the batter thoroughly.
♦ Lightly grease a large heavy frying pan with the vegetable oil. Place over a medium heat. Ladle 3 tablespoons of the batter at a time into the pan, spreading it evenly, and cook for 3 to 5 minutes or until the crêpe is solid but still slightly moist. Place 1 tablespoon of the tuna filling on the crêpe and fold it over. Remove from pan and set aside on a large baking sheet. Repeat the process until all the batter and filling are used up.
♦ Preheat the oven to 230°C/450°F/Gas 8. Place the baking sheet in the oven and bake for 8 minutes. Serve hot.

Holiday Fried Chicken

SERVES 8

This Italian version of fried chicken also makes an excellent starter or buffet dish.

1 tsp salt

½ tsp black pepper

¼ tsp ground nutmeg

¼ tsp ground cinnamon

½ tsp finely chopped garlic

2 small chickens, cut into small pieces

3 tbsp lemon juice

225 ml/8 fl oz olive oil

125 g/4 oz flour

2 eggs, beaten

In a small mixing bowl, combine the salt, pepper, nutmeg, cinnamon and garlic. Mix well. Rub the chicken pieces with the mixture and then sprinkle them with the lemon juice.
♦ Heat the oil in a large heavy frying pan over a moderate heat until it is very hot.
♦ Dip half the spiced chicken pieces in the flour and then in the egg. Fry, turning frequently, for 20 minutes. Keep the pieces from this first batch in a warm oven while cooking the remainder. Serve hot with lemon wedges.

Rice with Raisins

SERVES 6—8

This traditional Italian Chanuka dish originated with the Jews of Venice.

4 tbsp olive oil

450 g/1 lb rice

2 tbsp finely chopped parsley

2 garlic cloves, finely chopped

35 g/1¼ oz seedless raisins

70 g/2½ oz sultanas

¼ tsp salt

¼ tsp ground white pepper

950 ml/32 fl oz chicken stock

In a large heavy frying pan, heat the oil over a high heat. Add the rice, parsley, garlic and raisins. Cook for 5 minutes, stirring frequently.
♦ Add the sultanas, salt, pepper and chicken stock. Cover and cook over a high heat for 20 minutes. Serve warm.

Chanuka Fritters

SERVES 8

This baked dessert is distinctly Jewish-Italian.

40 g/1½ oz active dry yeast

225 ml/8 fl oz tepid water

350 g/¾ lb flour

½ tsp salt

150 g/5 oz sultanas

2 tsp anise seeds

1½ tbsp olive oil

2 tbsp lemon juice

450 ml/¾ pt honey

225 ml/8 fl oz vegetable oil

In a small mixing bowl, dissolve the yeast in the tepid water. Leave it for 3 minutes.
♦ Add the yeast mixture to the flour, salt, sultanas, anise seeds, olive oil, a scant tablespoon of the lemon juice and 125 ml/4 fl oz of the honey in a large mixing bowl. Mix with a wooden spoon into a soft dough.
♦ Place the dough on a floured surface and knead for 10 to 12 minutes or until the dough becomes elastic. Shape the dough into a ball and put it into an oiled bowl. Cover with a clean tea-towel and leave in a warm place for 1 hour. The dough will greatly increase in volume.
♦ Using your hands, flatten the dough into a sheet 1.5cm/½in thick and leave it to stand for 15 minutes. Cut the dough into approximately 36 to 40 squares.
♦ In a deep heavy frying pan heat the vegetable oil over a medium heat until it is very hot. Add the dough squares, 6 at a time, and fry until golden on each side, about 3 to 5 minutes per side.
♦ Remove the dough squares as they are done and drain them on absorbent paper.
♦ In a small saucepan, combine the remaining honey and lemon juice and bring to a boil over a medium heat. Cook for 3 minutes.
♦ Place the fritters in a large deep dish and pour the hot honey sauce over them. Serve immediately.

Italian
Yom Kippur Dinner

Yom Kippur, or the Day of Atonement, is a solemn fast day. A large
meal is traditionally served before the holy "day" begins at sunset, and
then a lighter, simpler meal is served to break the fast twenty-four hours
later. Challah, the traditional Jewish egg bread would be served (see
p.126 for a recipe). Dishes for both meals are given in this section.

Red Snapper Jewish-Style
Vegetable Cream Soup
Stewed Fennel
Cold Spaghetti with Brusco Sauce
Veal Escalopes with Red Wine
Fried Endive
Cinnamon Turnovers

Yom Kippur Bread

SERVES 8

This traditional loaf is served immediately after the holy day ends, to break the fast.

650 g/22 oz flour

40 g/1½ oz active dry yeast

225 ml/8 fl oz tepid water

350 g/¾ lb sugar

3 eggs

125 ml/4 fl oz olive oil

2 tbsp anise seeds

3 tsp vanilla essence

1½ tsp salt

2 egg yolks

In a large mixing bowl, combine 225 g/½ lb of the flour with the yeast, water, and 2 tablespoons of the sugar. Mix with a whisk into a smooth dough. Sprinkle with 50 g/2 oz of the flour and cover the bowl with a clean tea-towel. Set aside for 2½ hours.

♦ Add the 3 whole eggs, remaining sugar, olive oil, anise seeds, vanilla essence, salt and remaining flour. Mix into an even dough.

♦ Knead the dough until stiff on a floured surface. Divide the dough in half and knead each half for an additional 5 minutes. Let the dough rest for 5 minutes.

♦ Shape the dough halves into two 25 cm/10 in loaves and place them on a greased and floured baking sheet. Cover with a clean tea-towel and leave for 1½ hours.

♦ Preheat the oven to 190°C/375°F/Gas 5. In a small mixing bowl, beat the egg yolks with 2 teaspoons of water and brush the mixture over the tops of the loaves. Bake for 30 minutes. Remove and leave them to cool on wire racks.

Red Snapper Jewish-style

SERVES 8

This simple but delicious recipe is traditionally served to break the Yom Kippur fast. It has been part of Italian-Jewish cuisine for hundreds of years.

3 kg/6½ lb red snapper

60 ml/2 fl oz red wine vinegar

125 ml/4 fl oz olive oil

225 ml/8 fl oz white wine

600 ml/1 pt water

2 tsp sugar

1 tsp salt

2 garlic cloves, finely chopped

Clean and fillet the fish. Reserve the head and bones. In a saucepan, combine the reserved fish trimmings with the vinegar, olive oil, wine, water, sugar, salt and garlic. Cover and simmer over a low heat for 30 minutes.

♦ Strain the fish stock mixture through a fine sieve. Discard any solids that remain in the sieve.

♦ Preheat the oven to 220°C/425°F/Gas 7. Place the red snapper fillets in a large baking tin. Pour the fish stock mixture over the fillets. Bake for 30 minutes. Pour off the cooking liquid and serve in a gravy boat on the side. Serve hot.

Vegetable Cream Soup

SERVES 6

This delicious soup has a creamy texture yet uses no milk products.

3 tbsp olive oil

4 garlic cloves, finely chopped

1 onion, coarsely chopped

225 g/$\frac{1}{2}$ lb green beans, trimmed and quartered

175 g/6 oz peeled and coarsely chopped courgettes

175 g/6 oz peeled and coarsely chopped marrow

80 g/3 oz sliced carrots

175 g/6 oz peeled and cubed turnips

125 g/4 oz coarsely chopped celery

225 g/$\frac{1}{2}$ lb peeled and cubed potatoes

50 g/2 oz finely chopped leeks

50 g/2 oz finely chopped spinach

70 g/2$\frac{1}{2}$ oz cooked baby peas

175 g/6 oz cooked broad beans

125 ml/4 fl oz jellied cranberry sauce

4 tbsp finely chopped parsley

2 tbsp coarsely chopped fresh basil

1 tsp salt

$\frac{1}{4}$ tsp ground white pepper

1.4 L/48 fl oz water

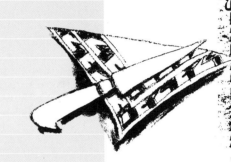

In a large saucepan, combine all the ingredients. Mash with a fork.
♦ Cover and simmer for 40 minutes over a low heat. Mash again. Replace the lid and simmer for an additional 20 minutes over a low heat. Serve hot.

Stewed Fennel

SERVES 6—8

The anise-like flavour of fennel is popular with all Italians, both Jews and Gentiles.

3 large fennel bulbs

6 tbsp olive oil

175 g/6 oz chopped onion

450 ml/$\frac{3}{4}$ pt water

$\frac{1}{2}$ tsp salt

$\frac{1}{4}$ tsp black pepper

Trim the fronds from the fennel bulbs. Cut the bulbs in half vertically, then chop each half horizontally into slices.

♦ Heat the olive oil in a large heavy frying pan. Add the fennel rings and onion and fry over a low heat for 6 to 8 minutes. Stir frequently.
♦ Add the water, salt and pepper and raise the heat to medium. Cook for 25 to 30 minutes. Serve with the cooking liquid in a deep dish.

Cold Noodles with Brusco Sauce

SERVES 6—8

This pasta dish is made the day before Yom Kippur and served to break the fast.

450 g/1 lb thin spaghetti, cooked al dente

125 ml/4 fl oz olive oil

2 garlic cloves, finely chopped

1 tsp dried rosemary

½ tsp dried sage

½ tsp salt

¼ tsp black pepper

1 egg

1 egg yolk

2 tbsp lemon juice

350 ml/12 fl oz beef stock

Put the spaghetti in a large saucepan of boiling water and cook for about 5 minutes until *al dente*. Drain thoroughly.

♦ Combine all the ingredients except the spaghetti in a small frying pan. Cook over a medium heat for 10 minutes, stirring occasionally. Reduce the heat to low and cook for an additional 5 minutes.

♦ Put the cooked spaghetti into a serving bowl. Pour the sauce over the spaghetti and toss well. Leave to stand for 10 minutes, stirring occasionally. Cover the bowl, chill for at least 1 hour and serve cold.

Veal Escalopes with Red Wine

SERVES 8

These delicate and delicious veal escalopes are quite simple to prepare.

50 g/2 oz flour

½ tsp salt

½ tsp ground white pepper

1.4 kg/3 lb thinly sliced veal escalopes

8 tbsp olive oil

2 large onions, coarsely chopped

3 garlic cloves, finely chopped

2 tbsp coarsely chopped parsley

125 ml/4 fl oz red wine

125 ml/4 fl oz sweet sherry

450 ml/¾ pt water

4 tbsp tomato purée

On a large ceramic plate mix the flour, salt and pepper together. Lightly dredge the veal slices in the mixture.

♦ Heat the olive oil in a large heavy frying pan. Add the veal, onions and garlic and cook over a medium heat for 3 to 5 minutes, or until both sides of the veal slices are browned. Remove the veal slices and keep warm.

♦ Add the parsley, wine, sherry, water and tomato purée to the pan. Stir well and bring to a boil over a high heat. Cook for 3 minutes. Cover and simmer for 10 minutes longer. Serve the sauce spooned over the veal escalopes.

Fried Endive

SERVES 8

This simple vegetable dish is a standard of Italian-Jewish cooking, and may have been borrowed by the Jews from the ancient Romans.

1.8 kg/4 lb endive, washed and trimmed
1 tsp black pepper
225 ml/8 fl oz olive oil

Cook the endive in a large saucepan of boiling water for 5 minutes. Drain well. Sprinkle the endive with the pepper.
♦ Heat the olive oil in a large heavy frying pan over a medium heat. Add the endive and fry for about 10 to 12 minutes, until the endive turns golden brown. Remove the leaves from the pan and drain on absorbent paper. Serve warm.

Cinnamon Turnovers

SERVES 8

Light and flaky, these turnovers are fairly complicated to make. They would be served before the fast begins.

350 g/12 oz flour
300 ml/$\frac{1}{2}$ pt warm water
125 ml/4 oz vegetable oil
1 tsp salt
125 g/4 oz softened margarine
450 g/1 lb sugar
2 tbsp cinnamon
1$\frac{1}{2}$ tbsp brandy
1$\frac{1}{2}$ tbsp Triple Sec liqueur
1$\frac{1}{2}$ tbsp water
2 egg yolks, beaten

In a medium-sized mixing bowl, combine the flour, warm water, vegetable oil and salt. Mix into a soft dough. Knead for 5 minutes and then set aside for 30 minutes.
♦ Roll the dough out on a floured surface into a sheet 2.5 cm/$\frac{1}{2}$ in thick.
♦ Melt the margarine and let it cool to room temperature. Spread a thin layer of margarine on the dough and dust with flour.
♦ Fold the dough to one third of its size. Wrap in clingfilm and chill for 20 minutes. Roll the dough out into a sheet as before. Repeat the process three more times, chilling the dough for 20 minutes each time. Roll the dough out into a sheet a final time.
♦ Cut the dough into 14 to 16 squares.
♦ In a small mixing bowl combine the sugar, cinnamon, brandy, Triple Sec and 2 tablespoons water.
♦ Brush the sugar mixture evenly over the dough squares. Roll up the squares diagonally, starting from one of the corners, into cylinders. Brush the egg yolks over the cylinders.
♦ Preheat the oven to 200°C/400°F/Gas 6. Place the cylinders on an ungreased baking sheet and bake for 20 minutes. Leave them to cool on a wire rack and serve at room temperature.

CHAPTER FIVE

Spain, Portugal
and the New World

Spain and Portugal   Jews first settled in Spain and Portugal in the first century CE. By the fourth century they were already beginning to suffer from discrimination. The Arab conquest of Spain in the eighth century was welcomed by the Jews, who subsequently enjoyed a period of enlightened prosperity. Toledo was the home of the largest and most influential Jewish community — by the twelfth century it numbered more than 12,000 members and had many synagogues. The city of Cordoba is remembered as the birthplace of one of the greatest Jewish literary figures, Moses Maimonides, who was born there in 1135. Jews also played an important role in Granada, Seville, the Costa del Sol, Madrid and Barcelona.

By the thirteenth century however, the Arab decline had begun and discrimination again arose. A pogrom in Seville in 1391 began a long period of persecution and enforced conversions, with many Jews in Spain unwillingly baptized and outwardly converted to Christianity. Many Jews continued to practise their own religion in secret, and were known by Christians as 'Marranos', from the Spanish word for 'damned'. From 1480 onwards, the Marranos became a target of the Spanish Inquisition — they were sought out and killed and in 1492 — the same year that Columbus opened the way to the New World — the Jewish community was officially outlawed from Spain and Portugal by the Edict of Expulsion. Tiny remnants remained, but 160,000 were forced to leave their homes.

The New World   Many fled to Italy, Turkey, Morocco and elsewhere in the Mediterranean, and later further north to France and Holland. But from the start, Jews also found their way to the Spanish- and Portuguese-speaking parts of the New World. The first synagogue in the Americas was founded in Curaçao in 1651, and three years later the first Jewish community in North America was established in Nieuw Amsterdam, now New York City. Thus the world-wide dispersion of Sephardic Jews was brought about — Sephardic comes from *Sephardim*, the Hebrew word for Spain, used to refer to those descended from the Jews of Spain and Portugal. Some Sephardic rituals, customs and religious observances differ from those of German or Eastern European — *Ashkenazic* — Jews. Sephardic pronunciation of Hebrew is different too, and is in fact the official pronunciation used in Israel. The Sephardim also developed a dialect of their own called Ladino or Ladismo, a combination of Hebrew and Spanish words similar in concept though not in sound to Yiddish.

The Spanish Jews never really recovered, although today there are active communities in Malaga and other places, and 3,000 Jews live in Madrid. But sizeable Sephardic populations are found throughout Latin America, including Brazil, Colombia, Argentina and Mexico, and there are large communities in Mexico City, Buenos Aires and elsewhere. Traditional Jewish cooking in Spain, Portugal and Latin America tends to be quite

similar to the local cuisine, with modifications to take account of the kosher laws. The recipe for paella given here, for example, omits shellfish. The modern Jewish population of the Spanish- and Portuguese-speaking world also includes many who fled from Hitler, bringing with them cooking traditions from elsewhere in Europe. Although no really distinct Sephardic cuisine exists, the dishes given here provide a broad cross-section of Jewish cooking styles in Spain, Portugal and the New World.

Jewish cuisine from Spain, Portugal and Latin America makes wide use of colourful local ingredients and traditions.

Holiday Fried Chicken ABOVE (OPPOSITE) *(page 167)*.

◆

Red Snapper Jewish-Style BELOW LEFT (OPPOSITE) *(page 170)*.

◆

Stewed Fennel BELOW RIGHT (OPPOSITE) *(page 171)*.

◆

Cinnamon Turnovers ABOVE *(page 173)*.

◆

Stuffed Mushrooms Provençal BELOW *(page 156)*.

Fisherman's Stew ABOVE *is a kosher adaptation of
the classic French dish, Bouillabaisse (page 159).*

♦

Chocolate Mousse BELOW *is an elaborate dessert
well worth the effort (page 161).*

Menu One

◆

Gazpacho
Sautéed Sherry Veal
Paella Marrano
Arroz con Pollo
Oranges Curaçao

◆

Gazpacho

SERVES 6—8

This chilled vegetable soup is delightfully refreshing on hot days.

2 cucumbers, peeled and coarsely chopped

5 tomatoes, peeled, seeded and coarsely chopped

175 g/6 oz diced onion

1 green pepper, coarsely chopped

375 g/13 oz coarse dry unflavoured breadcrumbs

3 garlic cloves, finely chopped

950 ml/32 fl oz cold water

60 ml/2 fl oz red wine vinegar

1 tsp salt

3 tbsp olive oil

$1\frac{1}{2}$ tbsp tomato purée

175 g/6 oz chopped onion for garnish

17 g/6 oz each chopped green pepper and peeled cucumber for garnish

In a large wooden mixing bowl, combine all ingredients except the garnishes. Mix thoroughly and then beat with a whisk until fairly smooth. Cover the bowl tightly and chill for 2 to 3 hours.

♦ Sprinkle the chopped vegetables over the individual soup bowls and serve.

Sautéed Sherry Veal

SERVES 6

225 ml/8 fl oz olive oil

150 g/5 oz green olives, stoned and halved

125 g/4 oz mushrooms, coarsely chopped

350 g/$\frac{3}{4}$ lb finely chopped onions

2 green peppers, seeded and finely chopped

4 garlic cloves, finely chopped

4 ripe tomatoes, peeled, seeded and finely chopped

1.4 kg/3 lb thin veal escalopes

125 g/4 oz flour

$\frac{1}{4}$ tsp salt

$\frac{1}{4}$ tsp black pepper

125 ml/4 oz dry sherry

125 ml/4 oz water

Heat half of the olive oil in a large heavy frying pan. Add the olives, mushrooms, onions, green pepper, garlic and tomatoes. Cook, stirring frequently, for 15 minutes over a low heat. Set aside.

♦ Dredge the veal escalopes in a mixture of the flour, salt and pepper.

♦ In another frying pan, heat the remaining olive oil over a low heat. Add the veal escalopes, in batches if necessary, and cook for 3 to 4 minutes per side. As the escalopes are cooked, set them aside in a warm place.

♦ Drain the oil and fat from the pan. Add the sherry, water and cooked vegetables. Cover and simmer for 8 minutes over a medium heat. Pour the sauce over the veal and serve hot.

Paella Marrano

SERVES 8

*In Spain there are literally hundreds of variations of this famous dish. This kosher
version uses neither pork nor shellfish.*

125 ml/4 fl oz olive oil

450 g/1 lb spicy kosher beef sausage, sliced

350 g/$\frac{3}{4}$ lb cubed stewing veal

350 g/$\frac{3}{4}$ lb cubed stewing beef

900 g/2 lb chicken, cut into small pieces

450 g/1 lb sea bass fillets, cut into small pieces

450 g/1 lb red snapper fillets, cut into small pieces

450 g/1 lb salmon steak, cut into small pieces

450 g/1 lb haddock fillets, cut into small pieces

450 g/1 lb mackerel fillets, cut into small pieces

1 tsp salt

$\frac{1}{2}$ tsp black pepper

80 g/3 oz finely chopped onions

1 green pepper, seeded and finely chopped

1 large tomato, peeled, seeded and finely chopped

4 garlic cloves, finely chopped

700 g/1$\frac{1}{2}$ lb rice

$\frac{1}{4}$ tsp saffron threads

1.4 L/48 fl oz boiling water

225 g/$\frac{1}{2}$ lb peas

In a medium-sized heavy frying pan, heat 3 tablespoons of the olive oil. Add the
sausage slices and brown well over a low heat. Remove the sausage slices and set
aside.

♦ In the same pan, heat another 2 tablespoons of the olive oil. Add the veal and beef
cubes and brown well over a low heat. Cook for 10 minutes after the meats are
browned. Remove from the pan and set aside.

♦ In the same frying pan, brown the chicken pieces over a moderate heat for 15 to 20
minutes, or until thoroughly cooked. Remove the pieces and set aside.

♦ Drain the fat from the pan. Add 4 tablespoons of the olive oil and heat over a low
heat. Add the fish pieces, salt, pepper, onions, green pepper, tomatoes and garlic.
Fry for 15 to 20 minutes or until the fish are cooked but still firm. Set aside.

♦ Preheat the oven to 200°C/400°F/Gas 6. In a large paella pan or flameproof
casserole combine the fried fish and vegetables with the rice, saffron and boiling
water. Stir well and bring to a boil over a high heat. Remove the pan from the heat.

♦ Arrange the pieces of sausage, chicken, veal and beef and the peas over the rice
mixture. Bake, uncovered, for 30 minutes, or until all the liquid is absorbed.

♦ Remove the pan from the oven and cover with a clean tea-towel. Leave it to stand
for 5 minutes. Serve with lemon wedges for garnish.

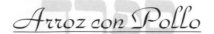

Arroz con Pollo

SERVES 8

Rice with chicken is a classic Spanish meal, hearty and easy to prepare. Serve it with a simple salad, a glass of wine and a simple dessert.

2 tbsp chicken fat
2 × 1.4 kg/3 lb chickens, cut into serving pieces
$\frac{1}{4}$ tsp salt
$\frac{1}{4}$ tsp black pepper
350 g/12 oz finely chopped onion
4 garlic cloves, finely chopped
$1\frac{1}{2}$ tbsp sweet paprika
4 ripe tomatoes, skinned, seeded and finely chopped
275 g/10 oz peas
$\frac{1}{2}$ tsp crumbled saffron threads
3 tbsp finely chopped parsley
700 g/$1\frac{1}{2}$ lb rice
1.4 L/48 fl oz boiling water

Melt the chicken fat in a large paella pan or saucepan. Add the chicken pieces, salt and pepper and cook over a moderate heat for 40 minutes. Turn the chicken pieces frequently.

♦ Remove the chicken pieces from the pan and set them aside.

♦ Add the onions, garlic, paprika, tomatoes, peas, saffron and parsley to the pan. Cook over a low heat for 10 minutes, stirring frequently.

♦ Return the chicken to the pan. Add the rice and boiling water. Stir well and bring to a boil over a high heat. Reduce the heat to low. Cover the pan and simmer for 40 minutes. Remove the pan from the heat. Remove the lid and leave it to stand for 5 minutes before serving.

Oranges Curaçao

SERVES 4

The first synagogue in the New World was built on Curaçao in the early sixteenth century by Sephardic Jews.

2 large navel oranges, peeled
4 tsp brown sugar
4 tbsp Curaçao or other orange-flavoured liqueur

Cut each orange into 3 mm/$\frac{1}{8}$ in thick slices and quarter each slice into wedge shapes. Arrange the orange wedges on individual serving plates. Sprinkle each plate with 1 teaspoon of the brown sugar and 1 tablespoon of the Curaçao. Chill for 30 minutes or until ready to serve.

Menu Two

♦

Avocado Soup
Turkey Mole
Refried Beans Jewish-Style
Grape Pie

♦

Avocado Soup

SERVES 6

Avocado soup is easy to make and provides an authentic Mexican start to a meal.

3 large avocados, peeled and mashed
2 tbsp lemon juice
$\frac{1}{2}$ tsp salt
$\frac{1}{4}$ tsp black pepper
$\frac{1}{4}$ tsp grated nutmeg
$\frac{1}{4}$ tsp cayenne pepper
1.5 L/$2\frac{1}{2}$ pt chicken stock

Combine all the ingredients except the chicken stock in a small mixing bowl. Mash to a smooth purée.

♦ In a medium-sized saucepan, heat the chicken stock over a low heat. Gradually stir in the avocado purée. Stir until the mixture is smooth and even. Bring to a boil and serve hot.

Turkey Mole

SERVES 8

The literal translation of the name of this recipe is turkey in chocolate sauce — which may sound a little odd! In fact, this authentic Mexican dish uses unsweetened chocolate and has a rich, cinnamon taste that is quite unusual.

3.6-4.6 kg/8-10 lb turkey, cut into 8 serving pieces
350 g/12 oz finely chopped onions
3 tomatoes, skinned, seeded and coarsely chopped
80 g/3 oz chopped sultanas
$\frac{1}{2}$ tsp ground coriander
1 tsp cayenne pepper
2 garlic cloves, finely chopped
$\frac{1}{2}$ tsp ground cinnamon
$\frac{1}{2}$ tsp ground cloves
80 g/3 oz finely chopped almonds
$\frac{1}{2}$ tsp salt
$\frac{1}{4}$ tsp black pepper
450 ml/$\frac{3}{4}$ pt boiling chicken stock
4 tbsp chicken fat
450 ml/$\frac{3}{4}$ pt cold chicken stock
40 g/$1\frac{1}{2}$ oz plain unsweetened chocolate

Place the turkey pieces in a large saucepan and cover with water. Cover the pan with a lid and cook over a high heat for 15 minutes. Reduce the heat to medium and cook for a further 45 minutes.

♦ Meanwhile, combine the onions, tomatoes, sultanas, coriander, cayenne pepper, garlic, cinnamon, cloves, almonds, salt, pepper and boiling chicken stock in a large wooden mixing bowl. Mix to a purée.

♦ In a large frying pan, melt the chicken fat over a low heat. Add the chopped vegetables and spice mixture. Fry for 5 minutes, stirring constantly.

♦ Add the cold chicken stock and chocolate to the frying pan. Cook for 10 to 12 minutes over a moderate heat, or until the chocolate has completely melted. Stir constantly until the chocolate is evenly distributed throughout the mole sauce.
♦ Preheat the oven to 230°C/450°F/Gas 8. Remove the turkey pieces from the pan and drain well. Pat the pieces dry with kitchen paper. Arrange the turkey pieces in a large baking dish in a single layer. Bake, uncovered, for 30 minutes.
♦ Pour the sauce over the turkey pieces and lower the heat to 180°C/350°F/Gas 4. Cook for a further 30 minutes. You can sprinkle the dish with sesame seeds before serving.

Refried Beans Jewish-style

SERVES 6

This Jewish version of the famous Mexican peasant recipe can be served as a side dish.

200 g/ 7 oz chicken fat
80 g/3 oz finely chopped onion
80 g/3 oz finely chopped green pepper
3 garlic cloves, finely chopped
1 tsp salt
1 tsp chilli powder
450 g/1 lb cooked pinto beans, drained

Melt the chicken fat in a large heavy frying pan. Add the onion, pepper, garlic, salt and chilli powder and fry over a medium heat for 8 to 10 minutes. Add the beans and fry for a further 10 minutes, stirring occasionally. Serve hot.

Grape Pie

MAKES 1 PIE

This Central American pie has a flavour similar to blueberry or bilberry pie, but is not as heavy.

800 g/1¾ lb large, black grapes
125 g/4 oz sugar
½ tbsp cornflour
60 ml/2 fl oz Triple Sec liqueur
1 tbsp melted butter
225 g/8 oz short crust pastry

Preheat the oven to 230°C/450°F/Gas 8. Peel the grapes, set the skin aside and discard the pips. In a large saucepan, mash the grapes to a pulp and bring them to a boil over a low heat.
♦ Strain the pulp through a fine sieve into another saucepan. Discard any solids remaining in the sieve.
♦ Add the reserved grape skins, sugar, cornflour, liqueur and butter to the pulp. Stir well and heat gently over a low heat for 3 to 5 minutes,or until the pulp is warm but not hot.
♦ Line a 23 cm/9 in pie dish with half the pastry. Fill the pastry case with the grape pulp. Roll out the remaining pastry and cover the pie, sealing the edges carefully. Cut steam vents into the top crust.
♦ Bake for 15 minutes. Reduce the oven temperature to 190°C/375°F/Gas 5 and bake for a further 40 minutes. Allow to cool before serving.

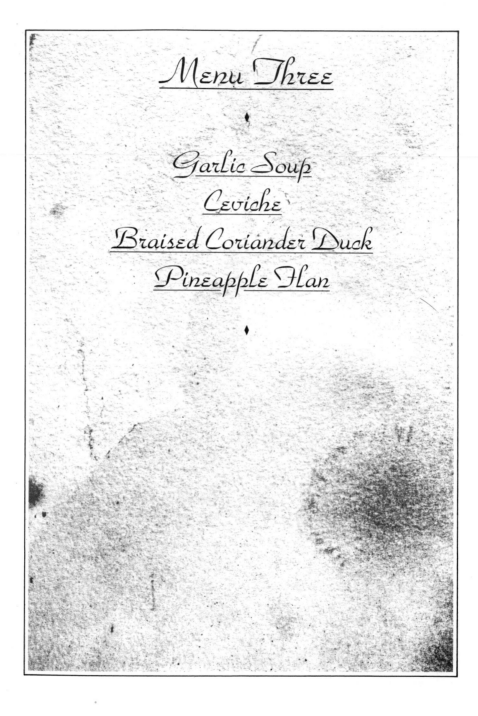

Menu Three

♦

Garlic Soup
Ceviche
Braised Coriander Duck
Pineapple Flan

♦

Garlic Soup

SERVES 6—8

Variations of this rich and tasty soup are found throughout the Spanish-speaking world.

125 ml/4 fl oz olive oil
8 garlic cloves
1 tsp paprika
$\frac{1}{8}$ tsp cayenne pepper
6 slices stale white bread, cubed
1.8 L/3 pt boiling water
2 tsp salt
1 tsp freshly ground black pepper
6 eggs, beaten

Heat the olive oil in a large heavy saucepan. Add the garlic and fry until the cloves are golden brown. Stir in the paprika and cayenne pepper. Add the bread cubes and fry until they are firm and golden. Carefully add the boiling water to the pan, making sure the fried bread cubes are not broken. Add the salt and pepper. Cover the pan and simmer for 1 hour.

♦ Slowly pour the beaten eggs into the pan, stirring constantly. Simmer until the eggs are firm. Serve at once.

Ceviche

SERVES 6

This dish can be traced back to the Peruvian Incas. The fish 'cooks' in the lime juice.

225 ml/8 fl oz fresh lime juice
225 ml/8 fl oz fresh lemon juice
4 dried red chilli peppers, finely ground
2 large Spanish or red onions, thinly sliced
2 garlic cloves, finely chopped
1 tsp salt
$\frac{1}{4}$ tsp black pepper
1.1 kg/2$\frac{1}{2}$ lb sole or plaice fillets, cut into 2$\frac{1}{2}$ cm/1 in square pieces
1 large head of lettuce

In a large glass or ceramic dish, combine the lime juice, lemon juice, ground chilli peppers, onions, garlic, salt and pepper. Stir well. Add the fish pieces and submerge them in the marinade.

♦ Cover and chill for 4 hours. Serve cold on a bed of lettuce.

Braised Coriander Duck

SERVES 6

The origins of this dish are hard to trace. It is served in South America, but seems to have a touch of Arab influence.

2.3-2.7 kg/5-6 lb duck, cut into 6 serving pieces and trimmed of fat
60 ml/2 fl oz lemon juice
$\frac{1}{2}$ tsp ground cumin
$\frac{1}{2}$ tsp salt
$\frac{1}{2}$ tsp black pepper
60 ml/2 fl oz olive oil
950 ml/32 fl oz light ale
450 g/1 lb rice
150 g/5 oz cooked peas
25 g/1 oz finely chopped fresh coriander leaves

Brush the duck with a mixture of the lemon juice, cumin, salt and pepper. Place on a plate, cover and refrigerate for 4 to 5 hours.
♦ In a large flameproof casserole, heat the olive oil over a medium heat. Add the duck pieces and brown them on all sides. Pour off all but 1 tablespoon of the fat.
♦ Add the beer to the casserole and bring to a boil. Cover and reduce the heat to low. Simmer for 50 minutes.
♦ Remove the duck pieces from the casserole. Set them aside and keep warm.
♦ Remove 700 ml/24 fl oz of the liquid from the casserole and bring it to a boil in a medium-sized saucepan over a high heat. Add the rice, stir, bring to a boil again and cover tightly. Reduce the heat to low and simmer for 18 minutes.
♦ Stir the peas and coriander leaves into the rice. Cover, remove from the heat and allow to stand for 1 minute. Arrange the duck pieces on a bed of rice and serve.

Pineapple Flan

SERVES 6—8

Popular throughout Mexico and South America, this dish has its origins in Spain.

300 g/11 oz sugar
125 ml/4 fl oz water
3 eggs plus 2 egg yolks
450 ml/$\frac{3}{4}$ pt condensed milk
350 ml/12 fl oz pineapple juice

In a small saucepan, bring 225 g/8 oz sugar and the water to a boil over a high heat. Reduce the heat to medium and stir gently. Boil for 10 to 15 minutes, or until the caramel turns a dark golden brown.
♦ Remove the saucepan from the heat and pour the caramel along the sides of a 1.4 L/48 fl oz porcelain mould, tilting the mould back and forth to get a thin, even coating. When the caramel begins to set, turn the mould upside-down over a sheet of greaseproof paper and leave it to cool for 2 minutes.
♦ Preheat the oven to 170°C/325°F/Gas 3. In a large mixing bowl, combine the eggs, egg yolks, condensed milk, sugar and pineapple juice. Beat until the consistency of the mixture is even throughout. Pour the mixture into the caramel-lined mould. Place the mould inside a baking dish half-filled with boiling water. Bake for 1 hour. Chill the mould for at least 3 hours.
♦ To serve, invert the mould over a dish and remove the flan by running a butter knife carefully around the edges of the mould. Serve cold.

Ceviche ABOVE is a Jewish adaptation of an
ancient Peruvian dish (page 189).

♦

Paella Marrano BELOW is a kosher version of one
of the most famous Spanish dishes of all
(page 183).

CHAPTER SIX

The English Speaking World

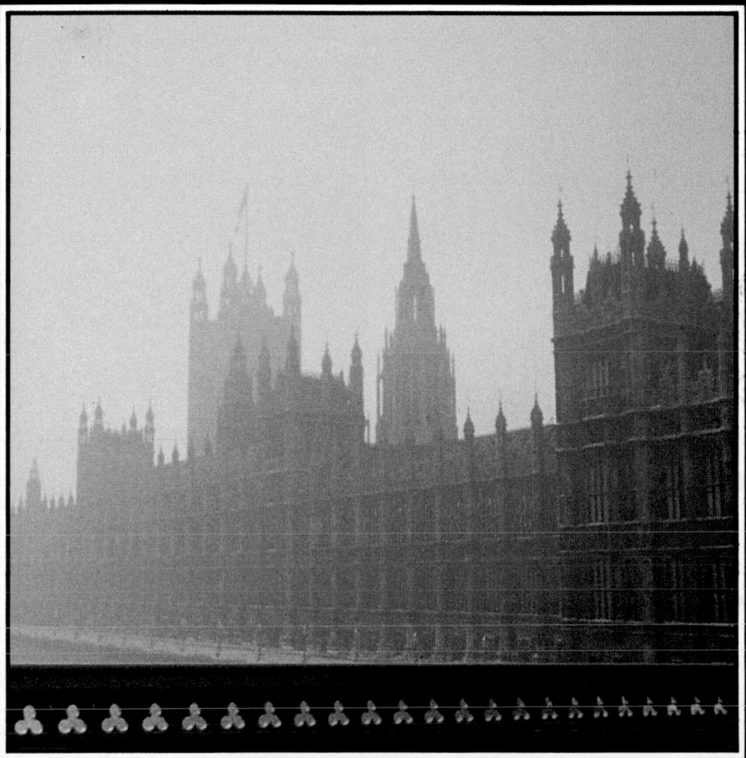

Britain Although there were already Jews in Britain, the expulsion of the Jews from Spain in the fifteenth century brought them in shiploads to the comparatively tolerant British shores. Queen Elizabeth I had a Jewish physician, and later, in the eighteenth and nineteenth centuries, many Jews rose to considerable prominence in British society. The British branch of the Rothschild banking house was highly successful, and one of its members was admitted to the House of Lords, while in 1874 Benjamin Disraeli, who was of Jewish descent, became Prime Minister. In the late nineteenth century thousands of Russian Jews fleeing Tsarist persecution also came to Britain, and today the British Jewish population numbers half a million, living mostly in London, Manchester, Birmingham and Glasgow.

The United States In 1954 American Jews celebrated three hundred years of settlement in the United States: the first Jewish settlers had arrived in New York from Brazil in 1654. One of the oldest Jewish cemeteries in America, founded in 1677, is in Newport, Rhode Island, as is the famous Touro Synagogue, which dates from 1763. From the beginning of the eighteenth century to the present day, North America has been a haven for Jews from all over the world. German emigrants arrived during the fifty years from 1820 to 1870, while a much larger influx of Eastern European Jews began in 1881 and continued until the outbreak of World War I. Today, there are over six million Jews in the United States. For decades the major port of entry was New York City, where emigrants were symbolically welcomed by the Statue of Liberty and officially processed on Ellis Island. Others arrived via Boston, Philadelphia, Baltimore and Montreal, and in the crowded tenements of New York's Lower East Side and elsewhere, they established vital, thriving communities. Yiddish theatre, Yiddish newspapers, synagogues, social organizations and schools all flourished in the unaccustomed freedom enjoyed by the Jews in North America.

Because the major waves of Russian and Eastern European migration have had such a profound effect on Jewish culture in Britain and the United States, people tend to think of their cooking as 'Jewish cooking'. And in America, of course, such 'Jewish' foods as kosher hot dogs and bagels have become part of the standard urban cuisine. The Jewish populations of both countries, however, have a wide range of origins, and their cooking has also been deeply influenced by the culinary styles of their adopted homes. For these reasons, no truly distinct British or American Jewish cuisine has emerged, and it is not really possible to present a typical British or American Jewish menu. Instead this section presents a number of favourite dishes from both Britain and the United States organized in suggested menus.

The Jews of the English-Speaking World came from all over the globe. Diverse cooking styles met here and merged to form a unique cuisine.

Sweet and Sour Salmon ABOVE *is a piquant dish
that makes an excellent first course (page 204).*

♦

Lox and Onions Omelette BELOW *served with
bagels makes a perfect light lunch (page 205).*

Menu One

◆

Scotch Barley Soup
Stuffed Kishke
Salmon Cakes
Liver Balls

◆

Scotch Barley Soup

SERVES 8

Glasgow has a large Jewish population. This dish is a variation of the popular Scottish dish.

80 g/3 oz butter or margarine
6 carrots, grated
3 onions, coarsely chopped
2 turnips, cubed
2.9 L/4¾ pt water
350 g/¾ lb pearl barley
1 tsp salt
black pepper to taste
chopped parsley

Melt the butter or margarine in a large saucepan. Add the carrots, onions and turnips and fry for 5 minutes. Add the water and bring to a boil.

♦ Add the barley, salt and pepper. Cook over a low heat for 2 hours. Stir in the parsley and serve.

Stuffed Kishke

SERVES 8

Probably of Eastern European origin, the recipe here is a British version of this famous dish. Serve slices of the kishke as a first course or as a side dish with meat or poultry.

1 m/39 in kosher beef sausage casing
125 g/4 oz sifted flour
50 g/2 oz matzoh meal
3 tbsp grated onion
1½ tsp salt
¼ tsp black pepper
1 tsp paprika
200 g/7 oz chicken fat
2 onions, sliced

Rinse the inside and outside of the casing. Cut the casing in half. Tie up one end of each half.

♦ Mix the flour, matzoh meal, grated onion, salt, pepper, paprika and 150 g/5 oz of the chicken fat in a large bowl. Stuff the casings with the mixture and tie up the open ends. Cook the kishke in a large saucepan of boiling water for 1 hour. Drain well.

♦ Preheat the oven to 180°C/350°F/Gas 4.

♦ Spread the remaining fat in a baking dish. Arrange the onion slices in the dish. Place the kishke in the dish and bake for 1½ hours, basting frequently with the pan drippings.

Salmon Cakes

SERVES 8

Strange as it sounds today, salmon was once a cheap fish, the food of the poor.

1.4 kg/3 lb tinned salmon, drained
1 tsp salt
black pepper to taste
150 g/5 oz chopped onion
225 g/8 oz butter or margarine, softened
50 g/2 oz flour
125 g/4 fl oz double cream
175 g/6 fl oz vegetable oil

Chop the salmon very finely in a mixing bowl. Add the salt and pepper. Add the onions, butter, flour and cream and mix until smooth. Shape the mixture into balls or cakes.
♦ Heat the vegetable oil in a large heavy frying pan. Add the salmon cakes and fry until golden brown on both sides.

Liver Balls

SERVES 8

This is a delicious variation on chopped liver, one of the classic dishes of Jewish cuisine.

20 g/$\frac{3}{4}$ oz chicken fat
2 tbsp chopped onion
225 g/8 oz fresh chicken livers, chopped
1 egg yolk
1$\frac{1}{2}$ tbsp potato flour
$\frac{1}{2}$ tsp salt
black pepper to taste
1 egg white, stiffly beaten

Melt the chicken fat in a large frying pan. Add the chopped onions and fry until lightly browned. Add the chopped livers to the onions and fry until browned.
♦ Remove the pan from the heat and stir in the egg yolk, potato flour, salt and pepper. Fold in the egg white.
♦ Bring a large pan of salted water to a boil. Drop teaspoonfuls of the liver mixture into the boiling water until all the mixture is used up. Cook until the balls rise to the surface. Remove, drain well and serve.

Menu Two

♦

Cream of Corn Soup
Sweet and Sour Meatballs
Barbecued Ribs of Beef
Bagels

♦

Cream of Corn Soup

SERVES 8

This classic American soup has gradually found its way into Jewish kitchens.

50 g/2 oz butter or margarine
40 g/1½ oz finely chopped onion
2 tbsp flour
950 ml/32 fl oz milk
350 g/12 oz cooked sweetcorn
1 tsp salt
black pepper to taste

Melt the butter in a saucepan. Add the onions and fry for 3 minutes. Stir in the flour and milk. Slowly bring the mixture to a boil and add the sweetcorn, salt and pepper. Cook over a low heat for 15 minutes.

Sweet and Sour Meatballs

SERVES 6

This dish is excellent for buffets, and also freezes well.

675 g/1½ lb lean minced beef
3 tbsp grated onion
1 egg
1 tsp salt
black pepper to taste
2 tbsp cornflour
25 g/1 oz margarine
1½ tbsp lemon juice
350 ml/12 oz beef stock
40 g/1½ oz seedless raisins
1 lemon, thinly sliced
2 tbsp honey
6 ginger biscuits, crushed

Combine the meat, onion, egg, salt and pepper in a mixing bowl. Shape the mixture into 2.5 cm/1 in balls. Roll the balls lightly in the cornflour.
♦ Melt the margarine in a deep frying pan. Add the meatballs and brown on all sides. Add the lemon juice, stock, raisins, lemon and honey. Cover and cook over a low heat for 35 minutes. Stir the crushed ginger biscuits into the sauce. Cook for a further 10 minutes.

Barbecued Ribs of Beef

SERVES 6—8

Barbecued dishes in general are enjoying a resurgence of popularity in America.

1.4 kg/3 lb beef short ribs, cut into 5 cm/2 in pieces
1 tbsp vegetable oil
1 tsp salt
$\frac{1}{4}$ tsp pepper
1 tsp paprika
1 tsp dry mustard
1 tbsp sugar
1 tbsp Worcestershire sauce
125 ml/4 fl oz tomato ketchup
125 ml/4 fl oz water
60 ml/2 fl oz cider vinegar
80 g/3 oz finely chopped onion
1 garlic clove, finely chopped

Preheat the oven to 180°C/350°F/Gas 4. Heat the vegetable oil in an ovenproof casserole. Add the rib pieces and brown on all sides. Pour off the fat. Add the remaining ingredients to the casserole. Cover and bake for 2 hours. Remove the lid for the last 30 minutes. Arrange on a dish with parsley and serve.

Austrian Bagels

MAKES 12 BAGELS

Historians of the bagel recount that in 1683 an anonymous Viennese baker decided to honour the King of Poland's favourite pastime, riding, by making a bread roll in the shape of a stirrup. The German word for stirrup is buegel — hence the modern bagel. The controversy over what makes a proper bagel continues to rage. But there is no dispute that the true bagel is boiled first and then baked, giving it a dense texture.

20 g/$\frac{2}{3}$ oz active dry yeast
350 ml/12 fl oz warm water
2 tbsp sugar
$\frac{1}{2}$ tsp salt
500 g/1 lb 1oz flour
2.75 L/5$\frac{3}{4}$ pt water

Dissolve the yeast in the warm water in a large bowl. Add the sugar, salt and flour and stir to form a soft dough.
♦ Turn the dough out on to a floured surface and knead until smooth and elastic, about 10 minutes. Cover the dough with a tea-towel and leave to rise for 15 minutes.
♦ Flatten the dough and roll out to a thickness of 2.5 cm/1 in. Cut the dough into strips 30 cm/12 in long and 2.5 cm/1 in wide. Roll each strip into a cylinder with a diameter of 1.5 cm/$\frac{1}{2}$ in. Cut each cylinder in half. Pinch together the ends of the strips to form circles.
♦ Cover the bagels with a tea-towel and leave them to rise for 20 minutes.
♦ Bring the water to a boil in a large pot. Preheat the oven to 190°C/375°F/Gas 5.
♦ Add the bagels in batches of 4 to the boiling water, reduce the heat, and simmer for 7 minutes. Remove the bagels, drain well, and place them on baking sheets. Bake for 30 minutes.

Menu Three

◆

Sweet and Sour Salmon
Vegetable Cutlets
Lox and Onions Omelette
Lemon Cheesecake

◆

Sweet and Sour Salmon

SERVES 8

A light and piquant dish that makes an excellent starter to a dairy meal.

3 onions, sliced
3 lemons, sliced
125 ml/4 fl oz honey
50 g/2 oz seedless raisins
1 bay leaf
8 thin salmon steaks
1 tsp salt
700 ml/$1\frac{1}{4}$ pt water
8 crushed ginger biscuits
125 ml/4 fl oz cider vinegar
50 g/2 oz sliced blanched almonds

Combine the onions, lemon slices, honey, raisins, bay leaf, salmon steaks, salt and water in a large saucepan. Cover and cook over a low heat for 30 minutes. Remove the fish.
◆ Add the ginger biscuits, vinegar and almonds to the fish stock. Cook over a low heat. Stir until smooth. Pour over the fish, and serve either warm or cold.

Vegetable Cutlets

SERVES 6

Kosher dairy restaurants are common in the Jewish areas of large American cities such as New York and Baltimore. This substantial dish is often featured on the menu.

25 g/1 oz butter
150 g/5 oz chopped onion
50 g/2 oz chopped celery
150 g/5 oz grated carrots
80 g/3 oz coarsely chopped cooked green beans
70 g/$2\frac{1}{2}$ oz cooked peas
3 eggs
1 tsp salt
$\frac{1}{2}$ tsp black pepper
3 tbsp matzoh meal
vegetable oil

Melt the butter in a frying pan. Add the onion, celery and carrots and fry for 10 minutes. Remove from the heat. Add the green beans, peas, 2 of the eggs, and the salt, pepper and matzoh meal. Mix well. Shape the mixture into 6 cutlets.
◆ Beat the remaining egg in a bowl. Dip the cutlets into the egg.
◆ Heat the vegetable oil in a frying pan. Add the cutlets and fry until both sides are browned.

Lox and Onions Omelette

SERVES 4

Lox is the Yiddish name for smoked salmon, and this recipe makes a perfect meal for a light lunch. Serve it with bagels in authentic Jewish style.

8 eggs
225 g/½ lb lox or smoked salmon, cubed
1 onion, finely chopped
black pepper to taste
4 tsp butter

Beat the eggs in a bowl. Stir in the salmon, onion and pepper.

♦ Melt 1 teaspoon of the butter in a frying pan. Add a quarter of the egg mixture and cook over a low heat until the omelette is solid. Repeat with the remaining egg mixture, making four omelettes in all.

Lemon Cheesecake

MAKES 1 25 CM/10 IN CAKE

450 g/1 lb digestive biscuit crumbs
225 g/8 oz unsalted butter, melted
1½ tbsp unflavoured gelatine
60 ml/2 fl oz cold water
300 g/10 oz sugar
5 large eggs, separated
pinch of salt
80 ml/3 fl oz milk, scalded
700 g/24 oz cream cheese, softened
80 ml/3 fl oz lemon juice
60 ml/2 fl oz orange-flavoured liqueur
½ tsp vanilla essence
finely grated rind of 2 lemons

Preheat the oven to 180°C/350°F/Gas 4. In a large bowl combine the biscuit crumbs and melted butter. Mix well. Remove 40 g/1½ oz of the crumbs and set aside. Press the remaining crumbs into the bottom and up the sides of a buttered 25 cm/10 in deep cake tin with spring clip. Bake for 12 to 15 minutes or until firm. Remove from the oven and cool on a wire rack.

♦ In a small cup, soften the gelatine in the cold water for 4 to 5 minutes.

♦ In the top part of a double boiler, combine 175 g/6 oz of the sugar, the egg yolks and salt. Beat well. Place over slowly simmering water. Add the scalded milk, a little at a time, beating constantly for about 5 minutes, until it is thick and smooth. Add the gelatine mixture and stir until dissolved. Remove from the heat and cool.

♦ In a large bowl beat the cream cheese until smooth. Add a small amount of the egg yolk mixture and beat well. Fold in the remaining egg yolk mixture. Add the lemon juice, orange liqueur and vanilla essence. Fold in until well blended.

♦ In a large bowl beat the egg whites until soft peaks begin to form. Add the remaining 125 g/4 oz of sugar, a little at a time, beating until stiff but not dry. Gently fold the egg whites into the cheese mixture.

♦ Turn the mixture into the prepared tin. Smooth with a rubber scraper and sprinkle with the reserved crumbs and the grated lemon rind. Refrigerate for 8 hours.

Holiday Recipes

Nineteenth-century ceremonial towel used at the
seder during the festival of Passover.

Blintzes ABOVE LEFT *are a traditional Shavuot dish*
(page 211).

♦

Hamentaschen ABOVE RIGHT *are served at Purim,*
either with a prune filling or a poppy-seed filling
(page 215).

♦

Potato Pancakes BELOW *are a classic of Jewish*
cuisine around the world and are traditionally
served at Chanuka (page 217).

Sabbath

At the beginning of the Bible we are told that God rested on the seventh day. The Sabbath — a holy day of rest, prayer and study — is one of the foundations of the Jewish faith.

The Sabbath, or Shabbos, is ushered in at sunset on Friday evening when the women of the household light and bless the Sabbath candles. After attendance at services, kiddush, the benediction over the wine, is recited and a Sabbath meal is served. Songs of praise, zemirot, are sung. On Saturday, the week's portion of the Torah is read at the synagogue. The day is devoted to rest and study. Shabbos ends at sunset on Saturday evening with the beautiful havdalah ceremony, where blessings are recited over wine, spices and a braided candle.

Because no fires can be lit or work done on the Sabbath, the foods served onSaturday are often either prepared the day before or cooked slowly over a very low heat starting late on Friday afternoon. Dishes which can be served hot or cold, such as kugels, are favourite Sabbath dishes.

In poorer households before World War II, the Sabbath was often the only time meat was served. A simple roast chicken is a traditional Friday night meal. Cholent, a slowly baked casserole of beans and meat, is traditional on Saturday among Eastern European Jews. Challah, braided egg bread, is virtually obligatory on the Sabbath whatever country you are in, as is red grape wine for the kiddush.

Petcha

SERVES 8

This traditional European Sabbath dish is often served at lunch. It can be made several days in advance.

1.1 kg/2½ lb calves' feet
4 garlic cloves
1 tbsp salt
black pepper to taste
sliced lemons, oranges or radishes to garnish

Clean and chop the calves' feet. Place them in a saucepan and cover completely with cold water. Add the garlic, salt and pepper. Bring the water to a boil, then cover and simmer for 5 hours.

♦ Remove the feet from the liquid. Remove the meat from the bones. Discard the bones and mince the meat. Return the meat to the liquid and boil for 5 minutes.

♦ Pour the mixture into a dish and leave it to cool. Cover the dish tightly with cling film or aluminium foil and refrigerate for several hours, or until the liquid has become gelatinous and firm. Remove any fat with a paper towel. Cut into wedges and serve garnished with sliced lemons, oranges or radishes.

Lokschen Kugel

SERVES 8

Kugel is a traditional Sabbath dinner dish, but can be enjoyed any time, served either hot or at room temperature.

4 tbsp melted margarine

225 g/½ lb thick egg noodles

salt

2 eggs

75 ml/3 fl oz honey

2 large cooking apples, peeled, cored and grated

2 tbsp lemon juice

80 g/3 oz seedless raisins

50 g/2 oz chopped walnuts

Preheat the oven to 190°C/375°F/Gas 5. Grease an ovenproof casserole with one tablespoon of the margarine.

♦ Cook the noodles in a large pan of salted boiling water until they are just *al dente*, about 5 minutes. Drain, rinse with cold water, and drain well again.

♦ In a large bowl beat the eggs and add the honey. Add the apples, lemon juice, noodles, raisins, walnuts and remaining margarine. Mix gently but well. Pour the mixture into the casserole.

♦ Bake until the top is golden brown, about 1 hour.

Shavuot

*Also called Pentecost, the Feast of Weeks, or the Festival of the First
Fruits, Shavuot is a harvest festival. It also celebrates the giving of the
Ten Commandments to Moses on Mount Sinai.
Shavuot begins on the fiftieth day after the counting of the omer. A
sheaf of barley, the omer, was presented as a sacrifice on the second day
of Passover. Fifty days after that, on the sixth of Sivan, in May or June,
the first fruits of the harvest were offered. Since the wheat crop was
harvested at that time, the sacrifice consisted of wheat bread.
Because Shavuot is an agricultural holiday, it is customary to serve
wheat bread and dairy dishes, and to decorate the home with flowers.*

Blintzes

SERVES 12

Today blintzes are served not only on Shavuot but as a Sunday brunch treat as well.

4 eggs
7 tbsp flour
$\frac{1}{2}$ tsp salt
225 ml/8 fl oz cold water
unsalted butter
For the filling:
450 g/1 lb cottage cheese
175 g/6 oz cream cheese
2 egg yolks
1 tsp vanilla essence
grated rind of 2 lemons
4 tbsp sugar

Combine the eggs, flour, salt and water in a mixing bowl until very smooth. Cover the bowl and refrigerate for several hours.

♦ Bring the batter back to room temperature. Mix again until it is very smooth.

♦ Melt the butter in a frying pan over a medium heat. Add a drop of batter to the pan. When it sizzles, the butter is hot enough. Lift the pan off the heat and drop 2 tablespoons of the batter into it. Swirl the batter around to coat the bottom of the pan thinly and evenly. Pour off any excess batter. Cook the blintz until lightly browned on the bottom, then turn and cook on the other side until lightly browned. Repeat until all the batter is used.

♦ To make the filling, blend the cottage cheese, cream cheese, egg yolks, vanilla, lemon rind and sugar in a mixing bowl.

♦ Lay a blintz flat on a floured surface. Place 2 tablespoons of the filling on the bottom half of the blintz. Roll up the blintz, tucking in the sides, into a rectangular, tube-like package.

♦ Melt some additional butter in the frying pan and add the blintzes. Cook on both sides until golden.

Cheese Kugel

SERVES 8

This sweet noodle dish is also served on the Sabbath. Serve it hot, chilled or at room temperature.

225 g/½ lb medium egg noodles
1 tbsp melted butter
450 g/1 lb cottage cheese
125 g/4 oz sugar
125 ml/4 fl oz milk
125 ml/4 fl oz orange juice
80 g/3 oz raisins
grated rind of 1 orange
2 eggs, separated

Preheat the oven to 190°C/375°F/Gas 5. Cook the noodles in a large pan of boiling salted water until they are *al dente*, about 5 minutes. Drain and rinse. Drain well.
♦ Mix the butter, cottage cheese, sugar, milk, orange juice, raisins, orange rind and egg yolks together in a large mixing bowl. Add the noodles and mix well.
♦ Beat the egg whites until they are stiff. Fold the egg whites into the noodle mixture. Fill a large greased baking dish with the mixture and bake for 20 minutes. Reduce the heat to 170°C/325°F/Gas 3 and bake for a further 55 minutes.

Russian Pirogen

SERVES 6—8

The filling for Russian Pirogen is generally cottage cheese or curd cheese seasoned with sugar and cinnamon or with onions, salt and pepper. In either case, these simple dumplings should be served topped with lots of soured cream.

125 g/4 oz flour
1 tsp salt
125 g/4 oz potatoes, cooked, peeled and grated
1 egg
2 tbsp water
125 g/4 oz butter
For the filling:
cottage or curd cheese
sugar and cinnamon to taste or chopped onion, salt and pepper to taste

In a mixing bowl combine the flour and salt. Add the grated potatoes and mix well.
♦ In a small bowl, beat the egg and water together. Make a well in the flour mixture and pour the egg mixture into it. Mix well. Turn the dough out on to a floured surface and knead well. Roll the dough out to a thickness of 7.5 mm/¼ in. Cut the dough into 8 cm/3 in circles. Mix the sweet or savoury filling. Put a spoonful of filling on to each circle and fold the dough over into a semicircular shape. Seal well, moistening the edges with a little water.
♦ Cook the pirogen in a large pan of boiling water for 5 minutes. Drain well.
♦ Melt the butter in a large frying pan. Add the pirogen and fry until golden brown on both sides.

Passover

Passover falls on the fifteenth of Nisan, in March or April. This most ancient of Jewish holidays celebrates the deliverance of the Hebrews from slavery in Egypt some six thousand years ago.

The Hebrews left Egypt in such haste that the bread they were baking had no time to leaven. During Passover, observant Jews eat only matzoh and other unleavened foods. All the everyday kitchen utensils and eating implements are removed and special sets used only during Passover are brought out for the eight-day holiday.

The first and second nights of Passover are celebrated at the seder, a ritual where the story of Passover is retold and a substantial meal is served, followed by Passover songs and songs of praise. Four cups of wine are traditionally drunk at the seder.

The matzoh plate and the seder plate are prominent on the table. The plate holds three matzohs, the symbol of Passover. In the course of the ceremony, the middle matzoh is broken and half set aside for the afikomen, or dessert. Perhaps as a device to keep small children interested, it is traditional for someone to attempt to steal the afikomen and then ransom it back so that the seder can end.

The seder plate contains several symbolic items that are referred to during the ceremony. These include charoses, symbolizing the bricks used to build the pyramids; maror (bitter herbs) symbolizing the bitterness of slavery; parsley, symbolizing spring; a shank bone, symbolizing the sacrificed lamb whose blood identified the homes of the Jews in Egypt, and a roasted egg, symbolizing the sacrifice in the Temple. In addition, a bowl containing vinegar or salt water is placed on the table to symbolize the bitterness of slavery.

Before the holiday begins, it is traditional to spring clean the household to remove all traces of leaven. It is customary for the head of the household to search the house the night before the holiday and find some crusts of bread that have been deliberately left. They are securely wrapped up and burned the next morning.

Traditional foods for Passover include a great variety of dishes made with matzoh, including kugels, cakes and pancakes of various types. Dairy products are traditional during the holiday, although the main course at the seder is often a substantial turkey or roast.

Charoses

SERVES 2—4

This mixture of apples, nuts, wine and spices symbolizes the clay the Hebrews used to make the bricks that built the pyramids. It is served at Passover with the bitter herbs as a reminder of the time of slavery.

125 g/4 oz walnuts, shelled
2 dessert apples, peeled and cored
125 ml/4 fl oz sweet red wine
1 tsp ground ginger
1 tsp cinnamon
2 tbsp honey

Chop the walnuts and apples together and combine with the wine in a wooden mixing bowl. Add the ginger, cinnamon and honey. Toss well.

Matzoh Brei

SERVES 2

A traditional breakfast during Passover. It can be made sweet by omitting the salt and pepper and substituting sugar and cinnamon.

2 eggs
salt to taste
black pepper to taste
2 matzohs, crushed
boiling water
25 g/1 oz butter

Beat the eggs in a bowl with the salt and pepper. Put the matzoh pieces into a small bowl and dampen them with the boiling water. Force the dampened matzohs through a sieve. Stir the sieved matzohs into the egg mixture.
♦ Melt the butter in a frying pan. Pour the matzoh-egg mixture into the pan and cook until lightly browned on the underside. Turn the matzoh brei over and cook on the other side. Serve immediately.

Chremsel

SERVES 4

There are innumerable variations of these matzoh meal pancakes. They can be made sweet or savoury, as one large pancake or several small ones. This version makes a number of small sweet pancakes.

4 eggs, separated
6 tbsp matzoh meal
125 ml/4 fl oz water
1 tsp salt
125 ml/4 fl oz groundnut oil

Beat the egg whites in a bowl until they are stiff.
♦ Beat the egg yolks in another bowl. Put the matzoh meal into a bowl and add the water, salt and beaten egg yolks. Stir and leave to stand for 5 minutes. Fold in the egg whites.
♦ Heat the groundnut oil in a large heavy frying pan until it is very hot. Drop tablespoons of the chremsel mixture into the oil and fry until brown on the bottom. Turn and fry until browned on the other side. Serve hot with sugar, soured cream and/or preserves.

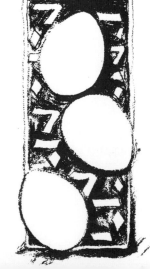

Purim

Also called the Feast of Esther or the Feast of Lots, Purim is a joyous holiday observed on the fourteenth of Adar, in February or March. It celebrates the deliverance of the Jews of Persia by Esther and Mordecai from a plot for their extermination by the evil Haman. The story is told in the Book of Esther. The scroll, or megillah, is read aloud. The children in the audience jeer and hiss whenever Haman's name is read. A seudah, or Purim feast, is served that day. Purim is also a time for festivities and gifts of food.

Purim Soup

SERVES 6

Traditionally served on Purim in Eastern Europe, this soup has a slightly sweet flavour.

450 g/1 lb beef brisket, cubed

2 beef soup bones

1 L/1¾ pt water

225 ml/8 fl oz tomato juice

2 leeks, white part only, cut into julienne strips

6 cauliflower florets

1 tbsp salt

2 tbsp sugar

1 tsp freshly ground black pepper

2 egg yolks, beaten

Put the beef, soup bones and water in a large, deep saucepan and bring to a boil. Cover and simmer for 90 minutes.
♦ Remove the soup bones and skim the surface of the soup. Add the tomato juice, leeks, cauliflower, salt, sugar and pepper. Bring to a boil, cover and simmer over a medium heat for 15 minutes.
♦ Put the egg yolks in a soup tureen. Remove the soup from the heat and slowly pour the soup over the egg yolks, stirring constantly. Serve hot.

Hamentaschen

MAKES ABOUT 75 HAMENTASCHEN

These filled pastries are traditional on Purim. As well as the traditional prune filling given here, Hamentaschen are often filled with either a prepared poppy-seed mixture called mohn or with any sort of preserve.

4 eggs

225 g/8 oz sugar

125 ml/4 oz vegetable oil

3 tbsp lemon juice

grated rind of 1 lemon

1 tsp vanilla essence

2 tsp baking powder

600 g/1¼ lb wholemeal flour

For the filling:
675 g/1½ lb prune butter lekvar
175 g/6 oz seedless raisins
125 g/4 oz chopped walnuts
grated rind of 1 lemon or orange
1 tbsp vegetable oil

Beat the eggs in a mixing bowl. Gradually stir in the sugar until the mixture thickens and bubbles appear. Gradually mix in the oil, lemon juice, lemon rind and vanilla essence. Add the baking powder and, mixing continuously, add the flour until a stiff dough is formed. Turn the dough out on to a floured surface and knead, adding more flour if necessary, until a stiff, non-sticky dough is formed.

♦ To make the filling, combine the prune butter, raisins, walnuts, citrus rind and oil in a bowl. Mix well.

♦ Preheat the oven to 190°C/375°F/Gas 5. Roll out a small piece of the dough until thin.

♦ With a 2.5 cm/1 in pastry cutter, cut circles of dough. Place one teaspoon of the filling in the centre of each dough. Pinch together 3 points on the circle tightly to make a triangle. Repeat with the remaining dough and filling.

♦ Place the hamentaschen on a greased baking sheet and bake for 20 minutes. Remove them from the oven and leave them to cool on the baking sheet for 15 minutes. Finish cooling them on wire racks.

Bean Cakes

SERVES 6

These Russian Bean Cakes are very popular at Purim.

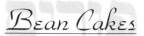

175 g/6 oz cooked black-eyed beans
1 tomato
1 onion
salt to taste
black pepper to taste
450 ml/¾ pt vegetable oil

Purée the black-eyed beans in a liquidizer or food processor until smooth, adding small amounts of cold water if needed. Put the purée into a mixing bowl.

♦ Purée the tomato and onion until smooth. Add to the black-eyed beans. Season to taste with salt and pepper. Mix well.

♦ Heat the oil in a large heavy frying pan until it is very hot. Drop teaspoons of the bean mixture into the pan and fry until brown on both sides. Drain on kitchen towels.

Chanuka

In Hebrew the word chanuka *means dedication. The holiday of Chanuka, which begins on the twenty-fifth day of Kislev, December, is also called the Feast of Dedication or the Feast of Lights. This eight-day holiday celebrates the victory of the Maccabees over the Syrians in 165 BCE and the rededication of the Temple, which had been defiled by the tyrant Antiochus.*

Chanuka is celebrated by lighting candles every night in commemoration of a miraculous flask of oil that burned for eight days instead of one when the Temple was rededicated. The holiday is also traditionally celebrated by giving children small gifts of money, called Chanuka gelt, and by playing games with a top called a driedel. In terms of Jewish history Chanuka is a recent holiday. In Western societies it has perhaps taken on disproportionate importance, particularly in terms of gift-giving, because of its proximity to Christmas.

Potato Pancakes

SERVES 4—6

This hearty dish, which has become a classic of Jewish cuisine around the world, originated with the German-Austrian Jews. Although most cookery books suggest that the pancakes should be served with a choice of soured cream or apple purée, connoisseurs know that they should be eaten with both.

Potato pancakes are traditionally served on Chanuka. This is probably because the oil they are cooked in is a reminder of the miraculous flask of oil that burned for eight days and nights when the temple in Jerusalem was rededicated by the victorious Jews in 165 BCE.

12 large potatoes
4 eggs
80 g/3 oz finely chopped onion
50 g/2 oz flour
2 tsp salt
225 ml/8 fl oz vegetable oil

Peel the potatoes and submerge them in a large bowl of cold water.

♦ In a large mixing bowl, beat the eggs and onion together. Gradually add the flour and salt, beating constantly.

♦ Drain and pat dry the potatoes. Coarsely grate them and drain them well. Press to remove as much moisture as possible. It is better to use the coarse side of a hand grater than to use a liquidizer or food processer, which make the potatoes too wet.

♦ Stir the grated potatoes into the onion-egg mixture until the mixture is evenly blended. Form the mixture into flat pancakes about 10-13 cm/4-5 in in diameter and 1.5 cm/$\frac{1}{2}$ in thick.

♦ Heat the vegetable oil in a heavy frying pan over a moderate heat. When the oil is very hot, reduce the heat slightly. Using a palette knife, put the pancakes in the oil and fry until they are golden brown and the edges are crisp, about 2 minutes per side.

♦ Serve hot with soured cream, apple purée, and/or preserves.

North African Chanuka Fish

SERVES 6

The Jews of North Africa have a distinct cuisine based on native foods. Any firm, white-fleshed fish can be used.

70 g/2½ oz cooked rice

50 g/2 oz chopped almonds

4 tbsp sugar

125 g/4 oz butter

½ tsp ground ginger

salt to taste

black pepper to taste

225 g/½ lb dates, stoned

2.7 kg/6 lb fish, cleaned

1 onion, sliced

1 tbsp cinnamon

Preheat the oven to 180°C/350°F/Gas 4. Combine the rice, almonds, sugar, 2 tablespoons butter, ginger, salt and pepper in a mixing bowl. Mix well. Stuff the dates with the mixture and close the openings with cocktail sticks. Pack the cavity of the fish with the stuffed dates.

♦ Grease a large baking dish with the remaining butter. Put the fish in the dish and top with the onion slices. Bake until the fish flakes easily with a fork, about 25 to 30 minutes.

♦ Remove the dates from the fish and arrange the fish on a serving plate. Arrange the dates around the fish and dust with the cinnamon.

Sephardic Date Cakes

MAKES 16

Dates are a staple food in North Africa and the Middle East. These cakes or menana are a traditional Sephardic treat on Chanuka.

350 g/¾ lb dates, stoned

225 g/½ lb butter

2 tbsp sugar

225 g/½ lb flour

60 ml/2 fl oz water

2 tsp orange juice

castor sugar for dusting

Soak the dates in enough cold water to cover for 2 hours. Drain well and pat dry with kitchen towels. Finely chop the dates in a liquidizer or food processor. Set aside.

♦ Preheat the oven to 180°C/350°F/Gas 4. Line a baking sheet with aluminium foil.

♦ Cream the butter and sugar together until they are fluffy. Gradually add the flour, water and orange juice. The dough will be quite soft.

♦ Shape the dough into 16 small balls. Make an indentation in each ball with your finger and fill it with ½ teaspoon of the chopped dates. Close the indentation and gently shape each ball into a round, flat cake about 5 cm/2 in across.

♦ Place the cakes on the baking sheet and bake for 30 to 40 minutes, or until they are lightly browned. Leave them to cool and dust with castor sugar.

Succoth

Also called the Feast of Tabernacles, Succoth falls on the fifteenth day of Tishre, in September or October. The holiday commemorates the period when the Israelites wandered in the Sinai wilderness and slept in booths, or sukkot. Succoth is also a harvest festival, as symbolized by the waving of the lulav — the palm frond — and the etrog — the citron. In ancient times, Succoth was one of the three pilgrimage festivals, holidays where it was the duty of all Israelites to attend services at the Temple in Jerusalem. The eighth day of Succoth is called Shemini Atzeret, or the Feast of the Conclusion. The day after that is called Simchat Torah, the day when the reading aloud of the Torah during the course of the preceding year has been completed, and a new reading begins. The American holiday of Thanksgiving was modelled on Succoth by the Pilgrims as they gave thanks for their first successful harvest.

Date and Nut Pudding

SERVES 6—8

This dish comes from the Russian tradition, but has a Middle Eastern flavour.

375 g/13 oz dates, stoned and chopped
125 g/4 oz walnut halves
80 g/3 oz flour
$1\frac{1}{2}$ tsp baking powder
$\frac{1}{2}$ tsp salt
3 eggs
1 tbsp sugar
whipped cream

Preheat the oven to 170°C/325°F/Gas 3. Grease a 23 cm/9 in square baking dish.
♦ In a bowl combine the dates, walnuts, flour, baking powder and salt.
♦ Beat the eggs with the sugar in a small bowl. Add to the date mixture and mix well. Pour the mixture into the baking dish and bake for 40 minutes.
♦ Serve warm with whipped cream.

Raisin Relish

MAKES 350 ML/12 FL OZ

This piquant, sweet-and-sour relish is typically Polish.

175 g/6 oz sultanas, chopped
1 scant tbsp chopped ginger
2 garlic cloves, finely chopped
$1\frac{1}{2}$ tsp sugar
$\frac{1}{4}$ tsp mustard seeds
$\frac{1}{4}$ tsp cayenne pepper
$\frac{1}{4}$ tsp salt
60 ml/2 fl oz white wine vinegar

Put all the ingredients into a food processor or liquidizer and process until finely chopped. Store in the refrigerator until ready for use.

Rosh Hashana

The Jewish New Year, or Rosh Hashana, is celebrated on the first and second days of Tishre, in September or October. It is a solemn holiday, for it marks the beginning of the Ten Days of Repentance that lead up to Yom Kippur, the Day of Atonement. The shofar or ram's horn is blown on Rosh Hashana as a reminder to the people of the need for improvement and atonement. Rosh Hashana is also a festive holiday, however, and large family dinners are customary. It is also traditional to serve sweet foods, such as apple slices dipped in honey, to symbolize the hope for a sweet year to come.

Mandelbrot

MAKES 40 SLICES

Literally 'almond bread', this Polish sweet keeps well when stored in a covered container.

3 eggs
275 g/10 oz sugar
225 ml/8 fl oz groundnut oil
3 tbsp orange juice
450 g/1 lb flour
4 tsp baking powder
$\frac{1}{4}$ tsp salt
4 tbsp crystallized fruit
125 g/4 oz chopped almonds

Preheat the oven to 180°C/350°F/Gas 4. Grease a 35 cm/14 in square baking sheet well.
♦ Beat the eggs in a bowl. Gradually beat in the sugar, then 125 ml/4 fl oz of the oil and the orange juice. Mix well.
♦ Combine the flour, baking powder, salt, crystallized fruit and almonds in a bowl. Add to the egg mixture and mix well to form a soft dough.
♦ With oiled hands shape the dough into 3 long flat bars the length of the baking sheet. Bake for 40 minutes or until lightly browned. Remove the baking sheet from the oven and cut the bars into diagonal slices about 2.5 cm/1 in wide with a sharp knife. Leave them to cool.

Teiglach

MAKES 30 CAKES

These sticky, deep-fried cakes are served as a holiday treat in Russia.

450 g/1 lb flour

2 tsp baking powder

8 eggs

450 g/1 lb honey

225 g/$\frac{1}{2}$ lb sugar

1$\frac{1}{2}$ tsp ground ginger

50 g/2 oz chopped walnuts

8 tbsp chopped crystallized fruit

In a large bowl combine the flour, baking powder and eggs. Mix well to form a stiff dough.
♦ Turn the dough out on to a floured surface and knead well. Roll the dough into strips 1.5 cm/$\frac{1}{2}$ in wide. Cut the strips into pieces about 2.5 cm/1 in long.
♦ Heat the honey in a saucepan. Add the sugar and ginger and stir well. Bring the honey to a boil. Drop the dough pieces into the boiling honey in batches and cook, stirring frequently, until the teiglach rise to the surface. Put the teiglach on a serving plate and sprinkle with the walnuts and crystallized fruit.

Rogelach

MAKES 36 CAKES

The dough for these cakes is quite rich. The cakes may burn slightly on the bottom, but this is an accepted part of the flavour.

125 g/4 oz butter

125 g/4 oz cream cheese

125 ml/4 fl oz soured cream

150 g/5 oz flour

125 g/4 oz chopped walnuts

125 g/4 oz sugar

1 tsp cinnamon

80 g/3 oz seedless dark raisins

Cream the butter and cream cheese together in a large mixing bowl. Mix in the soured cream. Add the flour and mix well. Divide the dough into two balls. Wrap each ball in clingfilm and refrigerate overnight.
♦ Preheat the oven to 190°C/375°F/Gas 5.
♦ In a bowl combine the walnuts, sugar, cinnamon and raisins.
♦ Roll out the first dough ball on a floured surface into a circle about 40 cm/16 in in diameter. Cut the circle into 18 pie-shaped wedges. Sprinkle the circle with half the walnut mixture. Repeat with the second dough ball.
♦ Starting at the wide end, roll up each wedge tightly. Curve the rolls slightly and place them on a greased baking sheet. Bake for 20 minutes, or until lightly browned.

INDEX

(Numbers in *italics* refer to illustrations.)

CREDITS

The publishers would like to thank the following for permission to reproduce copyright photographs: Jacket: Hing/Norton; pp. 6, 11 and 12 QED/Ian Howes; p. 8 David Burch; pp. 13 (top left), 151 (bottom right) The Jewish Experience; pp. 55, 122 (bottom) Moira Clinch; pp. 86 (top), 207 The Jewish Museum, New York; pp. 121, 123 (top, bottom left) German Information Centre, New York; p. 122 (top) Uta Hoffman; pp. 149, 150 (top), 151 (left) French Government Tourist Office; pp. 175, 177 (top left, bottom left) F. Ontañón; p. 177 (top right) Mexico Ministry of Tourísm; pp. 193, 194 (top), 195 (top left, top right, bottom left) British Tourist Authority, New York; p. 195 (bottom right) New York Convention & Visitors Bureau

Food styling pp. 15 (bottom), 16, 94 (bottom), 95, 145 (top), 146, 147 (top left) Any Pasco; pp. 14 (top, bottom), 15 (top), 51 (bottom), 118 (top left) Lynn Lazin
Special props courtesy Bronstein-Baskin Foundation, Libby Baskin, Francis Glic, Miriam Levy
Food preparation Janine Norton and Edward Hing
Special thanks to Mr & Mrs Gilbert E. Rosenzweig and Mr & Mrs Martin Burstein for use of silver and ritual objects from their collections